To sell is Human
Daniel Pink

Happy Selling!

Reggie Peere

Technology is crushing us, guys. It's disrupting how buyers buy and, therefore, how we sales professionals must sell. Buyers don't listen to us in the same way they used to because we no longer have power based on technical, product or current industry knowledge. All of that is right at our buyers' fingertips. We have got to change up our game. To succeed in this increasingly complex and competitive environment we need great presence. Sales professionals with great presence have the ability to read the situation and seamlessly adjust their behavior to authentically connect with their buyers. They are persuasive because they have genuine regard for their buyers, and convey a passionate belief in what they are selling. They do the following consistently and well:

- Tune in to their buying audience
- Connect authentically
- Inspire their buyers to take action

This book helps the reader understand what it means to have great sales presence, and why great presence transcends any sales process. throughout the book there are many practical skill-building activities, best practices, tools and templates to help you leverage your most powerful self to close more deals.

SELLING WITH PRESENCE

Use your personal power to close more deals

REGGIE PEARSE

Archway Publishing books may be ordered through booksellers or by contacting:

Archway Publishing
1663 Liberty Drive
Bloomington, IN 47403
www.archwaypublishing.com
1 (888) 242-5904

ISBN: 978-1-4808-4923-5 (sc)
ISBN: 978-1-4808-4921-1 (hc)
ISBN: 978-1-4808-4922-8 (e)

Library of Congress Control Number: 2017955092

Print information available on the last page.

Archway Publishing rev. date: 10/19/2017

ACKNOWLEDGEMENTS

Thanks to the people who helped me:

Amy Goldfarb
Dr. Herman Goldfarb
Dr. Ron Goldman
Linda Knox.
Dr. Jack McCarthy
Rita Burke
Garret Pearse
Trisha Zembruski
Michelle Booth

The shoulders on which I'm standing:

Bernie Cronin, who taught me how to sell.
Belle Halpern and Kathy Lubar, who brought leadership presence training to the executive suite.
Amy Cuddy, author of Presence: Bringing your Boldest Self to Your Biggest Challenges.
Patsy Rodenberg, author of The Second Circle: How to Use Positive Energy for Success in Every Situation
Mark Rittenberg, Corporate Scenes, the originators of presence training.

CONTENTS

Introduction ix

Chapter 1   Presence Transcends Process 1
What Is Sales Presence? 3
How Does Presence Transcend Process? 6
Three Ways to Improve Your Selling Presence 9

Chapter 2   Presence at the Center of the Sales Process 18
Applying Selling Presence to Process 21
Presence and the Sales Process 26
The Sales Process 28

Chapter 3   Presentations: Process and Presence 40
Behaviors and Skills for Presentations: Process 44
Behaviors and Skills for Presentations: Presence 47
Improving Your Presence 50
Exercises to Improve Your Presence 54

Chapter 4   Meeting Management 65
Your Presence and Meeting Management 67
The Sales Professional as Facilitator 69
Facilitation by Meeting Type 73

Chapter 5   Personal Branding 84
What Is Personal Branding? 85
A Two-Part Process for Building Your Brand 88
Your Appearance 100

Chapter 6   Your Social Media Presence 103
The Paradigm Shift in Buyer Behavior 104
Building and Maintaining a Social Media Presence 105

LinkedIn 106

Twitter 111

Facebook 113

Chapter 7   Be the Difference 116

Endnotes 121

INTRODUCTION

He was no more than nineteen or twenty, slenderly built, and clearly the outdoorsy type. I was observing him from halfway across the high-end outdoor-gear store. I was being part anthropologist and part protector. He was selling to my daughter, Anna.

On this particular Sunday morning, a quiet one at the local mall, my daughter was an ideal and rare prospect: a motivated buyer willing to spend hundreds of dollars on outdoor equipment for her upcoming trip to Asia.

From my "Dad-let-me-do-this-on-my-own" distance, I was quickly absorbed in the interaction. I sat watching the sales assistant—let's call him Shawn—connecting with my daughter, who often finds these kinds of interactions stressful. He was listening to her, educating her, and helping her make the right choices. What stood out for me was not so much that he followed a classic sales process (he kind of did) but more that he seemed to be doing everything in the right amount. He was the right amount of friendly, curious, confident, and passionate about the outdoor life. He quickly created a safe space for my daughter to talk honestly about what she knew and didn't know, what she thought she needed, and how much she hoped to spend. About an hour after we entered the store, my daughter and I left with our arms full of camping gear, hiking gear, and a survival kit. Anna was upbeat and excited, confident that she had made the right choices. And yes, she spent several hundred dollars more than she had budgeted!

On the drive home, I was silent, deep in thought, wondering why so many sales professionals have such a hard time being the right amounts. I have made many of the same wrong-amount mistakes in my sales career. It has included things like doing too much relationship building and not enough selling, too much talking and not enough listening, too much defensiveness and not enough curiosity.

"Cool guy," my daughter said out of nowhere.

"Yeah," I responded without needing any clarification about whom she was speaking. I thought to myself, *What a great sales presence.* He had made Anna want to buy without her feeling pressured to buy. He made her trust her own choices by supporting her with his knowledge and experience.

What Is Selling with Presence?

The world of selling has evolved very quickly in the last five years. We are in a new age of technology and consensus buying. Consensus buying means it's no longer a case of identifying and connecting with *the* decision maker in the room. There are, on average, 5.4 stakeholders involved in a B2B purchase. These buyers report they are having a harder time differentiating between the competing products and solutions being presented to them. [1]

Let's look at the dramatic role that technology plays in our buyers' (and our own) behaviors when looking to solve a problem or address a need. According to a recent study, buyers reported being nearly 57 percent of the way through the sales process before engaging a sales professional, regardless of the price point.

Here's the rub for those of us working in the sales profession: CEB's research also shows that sales professionals' selling behaviors are not evolving quickly enough to keep pace with their buyers'.[2]

What does this mean? It means that the product training you likely receive coupled with a robust sales process—the one you hopefully experienced during your sales onboarding—is no longer enough to arm you to successfully navigate a changed and still-changing selling environment. The traditional methodologies and sales processes don't work, because buyers are no longer using traditional methods to make purchasing decisions. The traditional methodology of matching solutions to buyers' needs is no longer a differentiator.

Our presence can be the difference. Successful sales professionals "become the value themselves, work with buyers collaboratively, and create real change for their customers."[3] Great presence means we have the ability to read the selling situation and seamlessly adjust our behavior to authentically and purposefully connect with our buyers. We are persuasive because we have genuine regard for our buyers and convey a passionate belief in what we are selling.

Our profession is becoming so demanding and competitive that we cannot ignore the research on the ways in which our presence influences others. For example, research by Stephen Porges, a behavioral neuroscientist of the Kinsey Institute, Indiana University–Bloomington, reports that as social animals, we are continually, as a result of our primitive origins, scanning for danger in our environments. Our nervous systems are constantly subconsciously working to co-regulate with those around us.[4] Translating this to a selling environment, a sales professional's ability to be calm, attentive, and warm is contagious. Negative states of mind such as being anxious, frustrated, or angry are also contagious. These emotions aren't always on display explicitly, but they're communicated in very subtle ways. The inference is that to be most effective in sales, we need to be conscious of these implicit states of mind and build a set of skills that enables us to show up in the right way and do things in the right amount at the right time.

This book is an exploration of what it means to "sell with presence." It will offer ways to create a personal brand that allows us, across all media, to use our *presence* to differentiate ourselves by authentically communicating our unique value proposition. We will look at the attitudes and behaviors that allow us to show up in the right ways across a range of interactions, including

- meeting a prospective buyer for the first time,
- presenting an insight or idea at a meeting,
- uncovering details and information about your buyers' needs,
- helping your buyers problem solve, and
- dealing with conflict.

You may be wondering what gives me the credibility to discuss this topic, so here's a little about me.

I was seventeen years old, sitting in my father's office, next to the sales counter of our family business. He was the fourth-generation owner of an auto-parts-distribution business. We were drinking coffee. The air was thick with the smoke from his cigar. "Any idea what you want to do when you graduate high school?" he asked.

"I want to be in sales," I replied without hesitation. I don't recall how I arrived at that answer, but I knew it was true. It was somewhat of a surprise to him, yet from then on he helped me set up informational meetings with sales professionals and sales managers in his business network so I could understand more about the choice I was making.

Not much more than a year later, I was eighteen years old, my father had died suddenly of a heart attack, and I had become the CEO of the family business, employing twenty people. The business was close to bankruptcy. I needed to learn quickly about business management, including an immersion into sales and sales management. I was fortunate to be surrounded by experienced and talented salespeople, and with their drive, commitment, and support, within two years the company was on a solid financial footing. By the fourth year, the business was the largest distributor in Ireland for a UK manufacturing company, Lucas Automotive. We also had the largest market share for a number of automotive- and agriculture-parts distributorships. My ten-year experience running the company began with a baptism by fire.

When I was twenty-eight, I wanted to do something new and different, so I sold the business and moved to the United States. My career in the States has included sales and sales-management positions in financial services, technology, and consulting. I have enjoyed success selling, reaching the highest ranking for sales in most of the organizations for which I have worked, and I have failed in sales roles. The experience of picking myself up, dusting myself off, and starting again is a familiar one.

Like anyone who has had a career in sales, lessons abound! Here are a few we all know:

- the importance of a disciplined approach to prospecting—however it is achieved—having the right flow of qualified leads into a pipeline is our lifeblood
- the grit, determination, and a little bit of luck that it takes to succeed in selling
- the idea that current success is no guarantee of future success

This book focuses on some of my other lessons and how they have shaped my development in the last twenty years. I have come to understand that the impact on my effectiveness as a sales professional is a direct result of my sales presence:

- I have learned to broaden my repertoire of behaviors and feelings, and I have learned when to more visibly show my emotions—warmth, excitement, frustration, or disappointment in the right amount
- I have had to let go of the belief that I needed to be the calmest, most in-control person in the room. (There is a time to be calm and in control, but not *always*.)
- I have learned "You get what you give." We are more likely to have buyers get comfortable if we are comfortable in our own skin, more likely to have them speak to us with vulnerability if we show vulnerability,

Having great sales presence will get you where you need to be. You will close more deals because you will have more credibility, trust, and better relationships overall.

CHAPTER 1

In this chapter I will:

- Illustrate why great presence transcends a sales process

- Define what it means to have sales presence

- Identify the characteristics, traits and behaviors of people with great presence, and what it allows them to do

- List the obstacles to great presence

- Describe three ways to improve your presence

PRESENCE TRANSCENDS PROCESS

Fourteen sets of eyes were on me as I plugged the cable into my laptop to begin my presentation at GE's corporate headquarters in Fairfield, Connecticut. I was with my head of engineering to sell GE our content delivery and streaming technology. We were excited to showcase to this audience our recently acquired capabilities for what we believed was the first time

We had been ten minutes late getting into the meeting room because a previous meeting had run late. So, I had the self-conscious experience of setting up while being watched by a slightly impatient audience. I glanced at the large screen behind me. It was blank. I pressed Fn-F4. Nothing. I did it again. Still nothing. A third time with a little more purpose from my stabbing finger. The screen remained dark. I knew that rebooting my aging laptop would take several minutes. None of the many career technologists present offered to help. My overly tight Windsor knot started to feel like a noose around my neck.

"Okay, this doesn't seem to be working. Let's just talk," I said. My heart was racing.

After going around the table and introducing ourselves, I asked my colleague, Peter, to introduce our technology.

With the blank screen as a backdrop, he began what became a thirty-minute monotonous monologue. It was every sales professional's worst nightmare. By the end, everyone around the table looked exhausted and bored, including me. I watched it happen and did nothing.

"Any questions?" he finally asked.

"How did you acquire your streaming capability?" asked a jaded voice from somewhere around the table.

"We purchased Prime Media Streaming several months ago," Peter answered.

People shifted in their chairs, sitting more upright and attentive. All of a sudden, we had their interest.

"Prime Media. Okay. Got it."

I identified the voice as Joe, one of the senior managers in the room.

"You guys know that Prime Media won the bid to live stream Jack Welch announcing his retirement and succession plan to GE employees globally?" he asked.

"Eh, no," I answered. I sensed the punch line was coming. I could feel the sweat start to dampen my back. Thank God I had kept my jacket on.

"Yes. And the first twelve minutes of his presentation, where he actually *announced* his retirement, were never streamed because some genius in your NOC (Network Operations Center) failed to launch the event." Joe had apparently fully recovered his energy.

My attempts to maintain a confident demeanor were betrayed by my eyes that would no longer hold a connection with anyone around the table. My shame only allowed me to make some clearly unimpressive pleas for leniency.

That was it. I stumbled over the finish line. "I promise to never let anything like that happen again on our watch if you give us this opportunity." Peter and I had been caught for not knowing this piece of information ahead of time and paid the uncomfortable price of trying to recover in a moment from what felt like a sucker punch. The Prime Media deal—a classic overpromise—was inked with GE before we acquired PMS. We were guilty by association.

So, we'd managed to end the meeting as poorly as we began.

What Is Sales Presence?

I have worked with salespeople, sales teams, and their leaders for over thirty years, helping them improve their sales processes and presence skills. The best sales professionals, those who have long-standing relationships and consistently successful careers, have traits and characteristics that set them apart from the rest of us. *They have great "presence." These people have the ability to read the situation and seamlessly adjust their behavior to authentically connect with their buyers. They are persuasive because they have genuine regard for their buyers, and a passionate belief in what they are selling.* They do the following consistently and well:

- tune in to their buying audience
- authentically connect
- inspire their buyers to take action

I have seen deals founder when the right technical skills were present—the GE story being an example—and I have seen deals succeed, facilitated by a sales professional with great presence who relied on others for greater technical knowhow. In fact, sometimes too much technical knowledge can work in opposition to the right presence, as the sellers are too busy demonstrating their knowledge and expertise to pay attention to the buyer.

What is your presence? Do you know? How do you make other people feel not just about you, but also about themselves when they are in your presence?

Characteristics, Traits, and Behaviors of People with Great Presence	What Great Presence Allows You to Do
❑ Comfort in own skin ❑ Projection of self assurance ❑ Relaxed alertness ❑ Making good eye contact ❑ Empathy ❑ Listening ❑ Curiosity about others ❑ Communication of values and beliefs ❑ Confidence ❑ Passion ❑ Boldness ❑ Expressiveness ❑ Authenticity ❑ Congruency of voice, body, and content	❑ Have self-belief ❑ Feel personally powerful ❑ Read the audience and adjust ❑ Establish credibility ❑ Be more creative ❑ Connect ❑ Engage ❑ Build meaningful relationships ❑ Show vulnerability ❑ Persuade ❑ Recover more quickly ❑ Be flexible ❑ Motivate ❑ Speak truth to power ❑ Influence ❑ Be trusted ❑ Inspire
Obstacles to Great Presence	
❑ Excessive anxiety ❑ Excessive stress ❑ Shame ❑ Negative self-talk ❑ Shyness ❑ Task orientation ❑ Workload ❑ Physical appearance ❑ Personal blueprint ❑ Lack of presence feedback	❑ Poor eye contact ❑ Rapid speech ❑ Wandering feet ❑ Tension in your face, eyes ❑ Stiffness and stillness in body language

Figure 1.

How Does Presence Transcend Process?

Throughout the book I will be breaking down all the components contained in the chart above. For now, let's look at how sales presence transcends a sales process. There is no doubt that as sales professionals, following a process in our interactions with buyers is a good thing. It provides structure to the meeting and can provide those in attendance with a context for why they are all seated around the conference room table or attending the virtual meeting. Having a prepared agenda, a time frame, someone in a facilitator role, and a set of meeting objectives are necessary components of effective meetings. However, these components of a typical sales process are not the artful magic that helps close deals. The magic is your presence—your ability to connect with your prospects and buyers in a way that makes them trust you enough to be transparent about their business objectives, challenges, hopes, and desires, makes them open to hearing your insights and solutions, and keeps them engaged as you navigate objections and negotiations. Your presence can create willingness to collectively and collaboratively work toward a mutually satisfying and profitable outcome. It's a quality of interrelationship that puts both buyer and seller, literally or figuratively speaking, on the same side of the table, working together to solve the buyer's business problems. It is the antithesis of the stereotypical salesperson that uses financial incentives and overpromises in an attempt to win the deal.

Most of us in sales have, at one time or another, been in a meeting where within the first five or ten minutes, our observations and instincts are telling us that the buyer across the table isn't engaged. Regardless, we press on with our process, determined to present our product's greatest features and benefits before the meeting ends, whether or not the buyer is interested in hearing them.

Early in my career, when I tried to sell this way, I would come away from the experience tired from trying so hard, and I would feel frustrated and demoralized. What I know now about meetings that go this way is that if I felt frustrated and demoralized, the probability is great that the people to whom I was trying to sell were having a similar experience.

When things don't go well, we tend to blame the process and other people. We say thing's like the following:

- We ran out of time before we had a chance to get their reaction.
- I don't understand why they responded so defensively to our insights about the future of their industry.
- They didn't seem engaged; in fact, they were kind of rude.
- Our SME (subject-matter expert) wouldn't stop talking.
- I asked some killer questions and got one-sentence answers.
- They didn't ask one question when we finished our presentation.

Instead, we need to ask questions like these:

- Did I/my team work hard enough to make everyone feel comfortable and invited to participate?
- How did I/my team show up in terms of our level of confidence and desire to engage?
- Did I/we respond in the right ways to both what was going on for individuals at the meeting and the collective dynamics of the group?

- Did I/we demonstrate genuine curiosity and empathy?
- Had I/we developed enough trust and empathy to have the buyer listen to my/our insights and ideas with an open mind?

When we can answer these presence related questions consistently in the affirmative, we will be successful more often than when we ask ourselves questions only related to process. Show up with the appropriate presence, and the process will evolve through your attentiveness, flexibility, and empathic facilitation. Meeting facilitation and presence is discussed in detail in chapter 4.

So, What Went Wrong at the Meeting with GE?

When you look down the list of obstacles to presence (bottom row of figure 1) the first four obstacles, excessive anxiety, stress, and shame that provokes negative self-talk were the striking culprits that underlay my poor performance that day. Those four obstacles became the barrier to many of the characteristics listed in the right column, What Presence Allows You to Do.

Excessive stress and anxiety, escalated by our late start to the meeting and the technology difficulties, left me feeling distracted and unable to connect and engage in a meaningful way. That, in turn, impacted my credibility with the group and therefore their willingness to trust me to make good use of their time. It all fed into a downward spiral of negative actions and reactions.

These triggers, or things that stress us out to the point of becoming a distraction, increased my heart rate and interrupted my ability to think clearly and imaginatively, be flexible in my thinking, or feel in any way powerful. Shame and negative self-talk, the close cousins of anxiety and stress in these situations, are potent enemies to presence. I experienced both of these emotions during the GE presentation. Couple that with our lack of research, a process downfall, and it was a recipe for disaster.

I'm using a somewhat extreme example to bring alive what happens to prevent us from being our most effective selves in every sales interaction. There are other triggers, including a high-profile finals presentation; a meeting with a buyer, the outcome of which could determine whether or not we make our quarterly or yearly goal; our self-belief overall; or issues in our personal lives. These things, if not managed well, can have a subtle and sometimes significant impact on our presence.

THREE WAYS TO IMPROVE YOUR SELLING PRESENCE

Depending on where you are in your selling career—your experience and what you know to be your strengths and challenges—there are some options to help you begin or continue your efforts toward developing or enhancing your presence.

1. Know Yourself

The foundation for improving your presence begins with increasing your understanding of who you are and how you show up in different selling situations. How you respond in a first meeting designed for discovery or a major presentation with multiple stakeholders or a highly charged meeting set up to resolve a conflict can vary significantly. Conflict resolution is discussed in chapter 4.

Self-awareness, as defined by the renowned psychologist Daniel Goleman,[1] is the ability to recognize and understand personal moods, emotions, and drives, as well as their effect on others. This is the critical foundation for establishing a presence that helps you to show up in the right way at the right time.

For sales professionals, self-awareness depends on our ability to monitor our own emotional state and to correctly identify it in any given selling situation. It is not just noticing our behavior, but becoming tuned in to the underlying emotions. As emotions drive behavior and our buyers respond to the ways in which we behave toward them, being able to tune in to how we feel will help inform the work we need to do to consistently behave in the right way. Here are some ideas on ways to build your self-awareness:

i. **Tune in to yourself** more often by consciously noticing what's happening internally. For example, as you wait in the lobby before your first meeting with a buyer, notice how you are feeling. Are you relaxed, appropriately stressed, or too stressed and distracted? Any number of factors can influence how you feel, such as your confidence level as it relates to your technical job skills, your excitement about the particular opportunity, how well you are doing against your sales plan, what's going on in your work or personal life, or how well you are sleeping. However you feel and whatever the reasons, start to notice it more. Here is where you can begin nonjudgmental awareness. Just notice your feelings and label them. You won't believe how this simple technique can begin to help you regulate your emotions and alleviate anxiety.

The corollary of how you feel and behave is how this influences the way your buyers feel and behave. As Daniel Goleman noted in his book *Social Intelligence*,[2] we have the power to influence the "emotional climate" of our interactions with others, both positively and negatively. So, start to tune in to how you show up and the effect it has on your buyers' behaviors because there is a cause and effect.

ii. **Ask for honest feedback** about your presence from people whose opinions you trust and respect. Receiving honest, constructive feedback and actually making changes in behavior can be difficult for many people. It can trigger us because it may challenge, as Doug Stone and Sheila Heen point out in their book *Thanks for the Feedback*, how we perceive ourselves.[3] It also can affect how we feel about the person giving the feedback, or perhaps we just don't believe the feedback is accurate. So, sometimes our initial work is to get better at actually being open to receiving feedback. I spent the first half of my career figuring this one out!

The source of the feedback can be a boss, a peer, a presence coach, or a loved one.

iii. **Take an assessment** that will offer insights on your personality and behavior style and how it is interpreted by others. There are many assessments available to help you build self-awareness. These include psychometric tests such as the Myers-Briggs Type Indicator, the DISC profile, and the Herrmann Brain Dominance Instrument. The results from these tests offer insights into your cognitive functions and behavioral style.

Another self-assessment specific to emotional intelligence is the Talentsmart EQ test. This test measures all four emotional intelligence skills: self-awareness, self-management, social awareness, and relationship management.

Psychometric tests like these are a popular and effective way to help you increase your understanding of what you do, why you do it, and how it may be perceived by others. For example, the MBTI test includes a measurement of where we lie on the introvert-extrovert spectrum. Since most sales professionals are extroverts, understanding how we are perceived by more introverted buyers can help us emphasize the behaviors that will allow us to connect with them more deeply. This might include being comfortable in silence. Long silences can sure freak a lot of sales professionals out!

More details about the above-mentioned tests are available online as follows:

MBTI
http://www.myersbriggs.org/my-mbti-personality-type/take-the-mbti-instrument/

DISC
https://www.discprofile.com/

HBDI
http://www.herrmannsolutions.com/

Talentsmart EQ
http://www.talentsmart.com/products/

There is a fee associated with taking these tests.

2. Improve Your Ability to Manage Stress

Long working hours, work overload, high-pressure deadlines and personal conflicts —sound familiar? There is irrefutable evidence of the negative impact sustained, excessive stress has on our brain function, heart health, and overall health. If you are reading this book, you are likely in a sales or sales-related role and don't need education on how stressful this type of work can be.

Not only does excessive stress have a long-term health impact, it also affects your presence. Because of the way stress limits brain function, your ability to listen, appear confident, empathize, and be comfortable in your skin is diminished. It would be great if you would consider some of the following ways to help you manage stress:

> i) Become a Corporate Athlete. Jack Groppel, author of The Corporate Athlete highlights the need to help people in stressful jobs improve their health and performance. He frames his work around the need to become a "corporate athlete." Corporate Athletes learn to be fully engaged in what matters, so they are able to perform at a peak level in demanding, high-stress situations. Groppel encourages us to build healthy practices into our daily routines and maintain a sense of control and balance in our lives. These practices include staying connected to our deepest values and beliefs, regular physical exercises, and identifying emotional, mental and spiritual objectives. His work highlights the need, above all, to manage and maximize energy—not just physical, but emotional, mental, and spiritual. [4]

For more on becoming a Corporate Athlete, go to www. hpinstitute.com.

ii) Practice meditation and mindfulness. This is a very effective way of restoring calm and inner peace. Meditation is considered a type of mind-body complementary medicine; it can produce a deep state of relaxation and a tranquil mind. During meditation, you focus your attention and eliminate the stream of jumbled thoughts that may be crowding your mind and causing stress. This process may result in enhanced physical and emotional well-being.

According to the Mayo Clinic, the benefits of meditation include the following[5]:

- gaining a new perspective on stressful situations
- building skills to manage your stress
- increasing self-awareness
- focusing on the present
- reducing negative emotions

There are many simple ways to begin this process. An app called Head Space is one of these. Check it out at www. headspace.com.

You can also learn meditation techniques from sites like http://www.artofliving.org/meditation/meditation-for-you/get-started-with-meditation.

iii. Focus on your breathing. Almost everyone in sales experiences excessive stress at one time or another—working to close the deal, meet your goals, the big finals presentation, and so on.

One of the most accessible and impactful of all relaxation techniques is diaphragmatic breathing, also called deep breathing or abdominal breathing. Breathing is something your body does below the level of thinking. Your autonomic nervous system is responsible for this, as well as your heart rate and thermo regulation. Breathing is the one aspect of your autonomic nervous system of which you can gain conscious control simply by bringing your attention to it.

In our stressful lives, most of us wind up "chest breathing," where the chest and lungs expand, but the expansion is restricted by tension and tightness in the muscles around the abdomen and ribs.

What can help us calm our nervous systems more fully is "belly breathing." This kind of breath comes from the abdomen and uses relaxed muscles to engage the diaphragm. When the diaphragm contracts, your lungs expand, pulling air in through your mouth like a bellows. When you breathe from your abdomen, your belly will expand and move out with each inhalation. Your chest will rise slightly, but not nearly as much as with chest breathing; your abdomen is doing all the moving.

This latter type of breathing is what stimulates the vagus nerve. A growing body of research conducted and reported by scientists including Stephen Porges of the Kinsey Institute, Indiana University Bloomington, shows the short-term and long-term benefits of stimulating the vagus nerve,[6] from staying calm to feeling safe in the moment and therefore able to remain present. It also influences the production of new cells and the repair and rebuilding of your own organs. Yes, deep breathing is that important!

3. Participate in a Sales Presence Workshop

Attending a training workshop to develop your sales presence is the ideal solution if you are looking for largely broad-based training with some individualized coaching help. The duration of these workshops ranges from two hours to two days. The breadth of the presence skills and behaviors taught and coached will be influenced by the workshop duration. The outcomes for sales professionals include some blend of the characteristics, traits, and behaviors of people with presence listed in the What is Sales Presence chart on page 3. A good training will address becoming more expressive, being a better and more empathic listener, projecting a sense of ease and poise when under pressure, and so on. You could also seek individual presence coaching instead of or subsequent to the presence workshop.

This is my only shameless self-promotion: For more information on how a sales presence workshop can help you, go to: www.sellingwithpresence.com. Most sales presence workshops will expose you to improvisational theatre. I write in more detail about the benefit of these theatre skills to selling in chapter 3.

Throughout the rest of this book, as I talk about presence as the force that can bring a prescriptive sales process alive or, indeed, render it obsolete, I will refer to the characteristics, traits, and behaviors of sales professionals with great presence and what it allows them to do. There are many ways to elevate your presence, some of which I have referred to in recent paragraphs. As you read on and the work necessary to obtain a great presence starts to come alive for you, refer back to the opportunities and activities available here and in other chapters, and decide which of them might suit you, based on your personality, your style, and your ambition.

Choose development opportunities that will challenge you and stretch you. I did, and at times it was somewhat excruciating—as I did my first improv theater scene, for example, but there is no doubt the payoff is worth it. Over the course of my several-decades-long selling career, I have come to deeply appreciate the value of this work. In the early years of my sales career, using meditation techniques or breathing exercises before a big presentation, for example, was anathema to how I perceived myself—a hard-charging, indestructible sales guy. It worked until it didn't. Then I had to figure out what was preventing me from closing the bigger deals or building and sustaining longer-term relationships with my buyers. So began my work on my presence. It hasn't been linear; the outcomes of what I did developmentally were never predictable, there has been a lot of fun and laughter along the way, as well as some significant growing pains, and the combination of all the work I discuss and skill-building opportunities I present in this book have made me a better sales professional and a happier person.

CHAPTER 2

In this chapter I will:

◆ Illustrate why presence should be in the center of any sales process

◆ Apply selling presence to a sales process

◆ Review a sales process and identify the ideal presence characteristics, traits and behaviors at each phase of the process, and what they allow the sales professional to do

PRESENCE AT THE CENTER OF THE SALES PROCESS

When I began my selling career, I was seventeen, selling alkaline batteries and flashlights by cold walking into small corner stores and asking for the owner. I was the son of the fourth generation of Pearse men who had owned W & C Pearse, originally a bicycle store, which had over time morphed into W & C Pearse, auto dealer and auto-parts distributor, and it was understood that selling should just be in my blood. It was much harder than I had imagined. I was nervous. I didn't know how to be friendly *and* sell something. Frequently, I didn't get beyond the initial small talk before thanking the bemused store owner for his time and walking out. Finally, one wet Friday afternoon, I made my first sale to an elderly store owner who sat so deeply in his chair in the corner behind the store counter that I had to lean over the counter and strain my neck to see him. I think he bought from me because I was one of the few visitors to his store that day. Two weeks after the order was delivered, he sent me a note asking if he could return the stock! In a terrible twist of fate, as I mentioned in the introduction, I became the owner of my father's business when he died suddenly at age forty-six. I had just turned eighteen. The desperate days of cold walking were over. I had unknowingly fallen from the frying pan into the fire.

For the next two years, as I actively ran the company, I was surrounded by experienced sales professionals who, when we attended sales calls together, did their best to hide their lack of respect for my inadequate selling skills. I knew I had much to learn. Two years later, when I saw an advertisement for a sales-training workshop being offered by a sales guru of the era, Zig Ziglar, I signed up, unsure what to expect. For two days, I sat in an auditorium with 499 other eager listeners as Zig Ziglar presented his process and selling techniques.

Late on day two, a Friday, Ziglar was presenting on ways to overcome resistance in a prospective buyer. He itemized a number of approaches, giving examples of how and when to employ each of the tactics. One that I remember well, for a reason that will become apparent, was to be certain to get a follow up appointment for a meeting with the resistant prospect—let's call him Fred. At the appointed time, the sales professional should stride confidently into the resistant prospect's office and declare confidently, "Today's the day, Fred! Let's get this deal done." That sounded workable, I thought. Take control of the situation, Ziglar told us. Save the buyer from himself, he exhorted.

The workshop ended Friday afternoon. I walked down the steps of the conference venue feeling excited and a little overwhelmed by all I had come to understand about selling. I bumped into Michael Hatton, who, for the last couple of years, had been trying to sell me a computer system for my business. I had told him I wanted to do it; I needed to—but it was a lot of money, and it was going to take a herculean effort to change from the long-standing paper-based system. I was twenty and had never done anything like it before. I was scared to pull the trigger. As we left the conference, we greeted each other with a little discomfort; we exchanged pleasantries and headed off to our respective weekend activities.

About two weeks later, as I was wrapping up the work week, Michael Hatton showed up at my office unannounced and asked to meet with me. I agreed to see him, and yes, he strode confidently into my office and declared, "Today's the day, Reggie."

I had two reactions in that moment. I thought, *You did not just do that!* And I said, "No, it isn't."

Over the course of that two-day Ziglar presentation, I learned the importance and helpfulness of a sales process, and in the moment that Hatton strode into my office I understand its limitations. I knew what he was doing, and it felt like I was being manipulated for his benefit, not mine.

There aren't many sales processes nowadays that advocate such blatantly manipulative approaches to selling, but over the course of my career, I have observed a mostly unintentional misuse of a sales process. What do I mean by this? If you are like me, you have probably seen and even done what stressed and strained sales professionals all too often do. We communicate in a way that does not demonstrate a genuine interest in the buyer as a person; we ask questions but our demeanor and our tone don't show genuine curiosity and interest in what the buyer has to say. We don't listen in a focused and empathic way that demonstrates sufficient care for the buyer's situation, and we often don't present our insights and solutions with a passion and belief that is sufficiently inspiring. Ergo, our presence matters—a lot.

Think how differently the conversation might have gone that Friday afternoon if Hatton had relied more on his presence and less on Ziglar's process. It might have gone something like this. With his demeanor and his tone, he could have shared some of his concerns and shown a genuine interest in what was preventing me from doing the deal. He could have connected and empathized with me. Such an approach would have sounded more like, "You've had a lot on your plate since your dad died. I can totally understand that making big changes might be difficult. We've been talking for a couple of years now about installing our computer system. I know you have spoken about the value you see in our system. Would you be willing to discuss what's preventing you from making a decision to move forward?" Those words, said with sincerity and authenticity, would have yielded important information, such as my need for reassurance about the ROI and having the necessary support during the implementation phase—certainly much more useful information for Hatton than my blurted "No, it isn't."

APPLYING SELLING PRESENCE TO PROCESS

Some people are seemingly born with great presence; the rest of us have to work at it. Our tendency is to write ourselves off in comparison to these people, believing that such charismatic and comfortably outgoing people are born that way. Lucky them to have such magnetic and compelling energy! In fact, we are all born with this energy. Unfortunately, many of us lose it, or it becomes depleted along the way for reasons including enculturation, how we are socialized in our family of origin, or through life events. It gets squeezed out of us. All you have to do to understand this is observe toddlers and see their expressive energy, and their ease and natural comfort in their own skins. And this includes apparently shy babies. This book will help you embrace your presence more fully or, if necessary, reclaim it. What follows is an overview of the foundational underpinnings of great selling presence in the context of my experience with Michael Hatton. These are being self-aware, reading your buyer audience and responding appropriately, and connecting and empathizing.

1. Be self-aware. We need to be particularly attentive to what's going on for us when things are not going the way we would have wished or hoped. It's under these circumstances that our behavior can be less than optimal.

Increased self-awareness for Michael Hatton would have helped him understand how his impatience and frustration with how long the deal was taking impacted his behavior—an impatience, I discovered later, born of the pressure being put on him by his boss to close a deal with my company. It would have been the first deal in our space for them, which would have given them a reference site for future deals.

Rather than aligning with me, the buyer, his behavior caused him to push to get the deal done for his sake rather than both of our sakes.

Think about all the possible scenes, from the first interaction with a prospective buyer virtually or at a face-to-face meeting to the critical moments in the final negotiation, the outcome of which could determine whether you make your monthly, quarterly, or annual sales goal. Sales professionals can experience a plethora of emotions from the beginning of the sales cycle to the end and even from one end of the day to the other. The emotions on the negative end of the spectrum—frustration, anger, disappointment—can cause us to strain a little too much trying to close the sale before the buyer is ready. We can help manage these feelings by simply noticing them, labeling them correctly and allowing ourselves, for a few minutes, to just notice them and how they make our body feel. My usual tendency was to try to push them away, ignore them and plow through them.

Think about the excitement of getting the first meeting with a targeted buyer, the stress of being bullied by a powerful decision maker, the frustration of dealing with procurement, leading to the joy of closing the deal. These emotions can be experienced during the sales cycle with a single buyer or throughout a day with a range of buyers. That's why a career in sales is not for the faint of heart!

2. Read your buyer audience and respond appropriately. I was clearly ill at ease with the decision to purchase a computer system for my company. I was young and obviously hadn't made many deals of this size and significance before. I'm sure as I sit here remembering it, everything about me conveyed my resistance—my tone, facial expression, body language. It was a big change for a business that had done things the same way for a long time. If only Hatton had been relaxed enough himself to notice these signals, and empathic enough to respond to them.

Wouldn't it be wonderful if every sales interaction was with a relaxed, happy, and transparent buyer whose prime goal was to work hard to make a mutually beneficial partnership happen? They're out there, but mostly, buyer to buyer and meeting to meeting, the mood, behavior, verbal and nonverbal cues vary, sometimes subtly and sometimes in quite jarring ways.

Reading our buyer audience and responding appropriately needs to happen at a number of different levels. There is a part of our brain that automatically and compulsively scans everyone we encounter to determine whether they are to be trusted. At this level, our brain is asking, *Is this person safe? Can I count on him or her?*[1] Sometimes we are conscious of this happening; it also continues outside of our awareness. At a first meeting with a new buyer, that instinct may be heightened on both sides of the table.

Reading the audience needs to happen at a macro and micro level. At the macro level, it's about noting the overall energy and mood in the room. Is the buyer attentive? Does he or she seem engaged and engaging? At the micro level, it's about observing and responding to the individuals' levels of apparent engagement and reactions. Do they look and sound interested? Is he or she bored? Our job is to gauge the presence of those to whom we are trying to sell.

3. Connect and empathize. It was a moment in the sales process when it was important for Hatton to connect with me, be genuinely curious about what was preventing me from making the decision, and demonstrate his willingness to help and support me. Sometimes it's that simple—and that difficult, because of competing agendas—yours and the buyer's.

E. M. Forster, the great British writer, famously once wrote, "Only connect." The core human task, he is saying, the absolute essential requirement for human beings, is that they form powerful connections. People are inspired to achieve great things when they form powerful connections with each other.

Now, in the above sentence, replace "human/human beings" with "sales professionals," and you have a battle cry for what is at the core of a sales professional's work. Whether you are using the more traditional consultative orientation with your buyers or the more contemporary insight-led approach, the quality of the connection you establish, all other things being equal, will be the difference between success and failure.

A prime objective of the sales professional's effort is to create "psychological safety" for the buyer. Harvard Business School professor Amy Edmonson coined the term. She defines it as a belief that one will not be punished or humiliated for speaking up with ideas, questions, or concerns.[2]

I'm borrowing her term and applying it to the dynamics of selling situations because when we create such "safety" with a buyer, we have a true sense of being in it together, mutual respect, a desire to learn and improve, curiosity, and vulnerability. We don't have the luxury of getting here with all of our prospects and buyers, but when we do, it is both relationally and financially rewarding.

How to Connect and Empathize: Begin with your orientation. Austrian-born philosopher Martin Buber wrote that we can adopt two attitudes toward others: I-Thou or I-It.[3] He wrote that I-Thou is a relationship of mutuality and reciprocity, while I-It is a relationship of separateness, where we view the other as something to be utilized. We don't necessarily see them or their needs. Rather, we see them only in terms of how they can be utilized in satisfying our own needs such as closing a deal, making our sales goal or earning a commission.

So, when we find ourselves thinking more about the revenue or commission, the praise or promotion we'll get if we close the deal, then we are I-It oriented. The first person to notice when we're not in it for them or with them is our prospect or buyer.

There is no doubt I have been guilty of doing the commission calculation in my head after the opportunity has been scoped or getting excited about making my sales quota as I wrote the initial proposal. *Too soon*, I hear you say! Yes, it is. Though I'd argue it's only harmful when those thoughts influence our presence in a harmful way. For example, a buyer told me this story about a former colleague of mine—a person I had introduced to the buyer. After an initial meeting, the buyer told my ex-colleague that, though she would be interested in a demo of his product sometime in the future, she had no immediate opportunities for him to work with her organization. Yet, for several weeks after the meeting, this sales professional continued to call and e-mail her excessively. Unfortunately, he was way behind on his business plan. This seasoned sales professional had a poor presence in the eyes of the buyer. She wasn't exactly ecstatic with me for making the introduction.

On the flip side, a sales professional who spent many years as one of the top radio sales producers in the Boston market recounted the times when she was at her best. She said, "I felt like I was completely in it with the client. I wasn't thinking about anything except what the problem was that the client needed to solve and how we, together, could get it done. These were always exhilarating moments for me. My financial reward was a natural outcome of me working at my best. It was never the primary or even secondary motivation in those moments."

At its best, the sales process is a map that helps guide us through an interaction or series of interactions with our buyers as we explore an opportunity to do business. However, it is rarely a simple matter of moving in a linear fashion from first exploratory meeting, to presentation, to close. Your presence, including your relational skills, credibility, power of persuasion, and the ability to keep putting your best foot forward, will more positively influence the outcome of the sales effort.

PRESENCE AND THE SALES PROCESS

What follows are some thoughts and suggestions about the most effective presence for a sales professional contingent on where you are in relationship to your buyer and where you are in the sales cycle. If it is a new relationship and a new opportunity, the focus of your effort should be on connecting with the buyer at a human level. It is about behaving in a way that communicates openness on your part and a genuine desire *to connect* with them.

This orientation should never take a backseat in a relationship, but in the early exchanges, particularly in a new-buyer relationship, it is often those blink moments that can determine the relational path that's taken. Research has proven that we seldom, as the adage goes, get a second chance to make a first impression.[4]

As you move through the exploration of the buyer's situation, your presence should be guided by a *genuine curiosity* to understand all you can about what problems they are trying to solve or the opportunities they are pursuing at an organizational, business unit, or personal level, whatever the case may be. I emphasize genuine curiosity coupled with the discipline of listening to fully understand. It is this *quality of presence* that will truly differentiate the great from the average. What this means is it's not about getting bent out of shape trying to wordsmith a so-called killer question. Rather, it's about asking the appropriate questions and conveying authentically through tone, body language, and facial expressions, your genuine interest.

Whether you are presenting a solution, offering an idea, or bringing an insight to a buyer, it is all about conveying your *passion* for what you are selling. Presentations are, content-wise, the comfort zone for sales professionals. However, your presence through *tone, vocal variety, expressiveness, and self-confidence* is arguably going to be the difference between being average and being better than the rest.

When dealing with buyer resistance or objections to your proposed solution, your ability to stay fully present is, for most sales professionals, the biggest challenge. At the very moment we need it the most, our best, most present self, seems to sense a threat and then deserts us. Staying present in such moments means not going on the attack or getting defensive or becoming passive. It is about remaining attentive to the buyer and managing our default physiological responses, so that we can stay engaged in the conversation and connected to the buyer.

There is no one best sales process. In fact, many sales processes taught by sales-training companies, broadly speaking, differ only in the language they use: pain versus needs, benefit versus value, positioning versus rapport building, for example. Whatever process you have adopted as your own, if it works for you, keep doing it. What will make the difference for you is how well you bring your presence to bear on your adopted process. Having great presence means having the poise, self-assurance, empathy, authenticity, and flexibility to stay in the game, even when the odds seem stacked against us.

THE SALES PROCESS

Over the course of my selling and sales-training career, I have experienced or been exposed to about a half dozen sales processes and methodologies.

Generically, sales processes are broadly divided into the following phases: **opening, discovery, presentation, managing resistance**, and **close**. This can happen at one meeting but more likely over the course of a series of meetings.

Here I am going to go into more detail on each phase of a sales process. I also tie presence characteristics, traits and behaviors to each of the phases.

1. **Opening Phase**

During the opening phase of a sales interaction, the focus is on making personal connections by getting to know or reconnecting with the people at the meeting. It's also about creating the parameters and objectives of the meeting: the agenda and time, and the individual and collective desired outcomes.

It is the sales professional's role to lead the meeting if he or she sought the meeting. If the buyer requested the meeting, it must be made explicit who will be leading it. This leadership or facilitator role includes setting the tone, structure, and direction of the meeting. Meeting management is discussed in detail in chapter 4.

Ideally, the opening phase includes the following:

- *Creating a space* for casual conversation to occur. This can happen on the walk from the reception area, for example, or as people settle into their places around the conference room table.
- *Itemizing the agenda* item or items that will be discussed during the meeting. Whether or not you have already sent an e-mail before the meeting, it is important to review the agenda at the beginning, to make sure everyone is in agreement as to the purpose of the meeting.
- *Introducing the people* from the sales professional's organization. This is a brief overview of who you are and who you have brought to the meeting, if you have invited others. It is also helpful to highlight the reason you have brought an additional resource, by explaining the value he or she will bring to the meeting. This may be done by the sales professional, or she may invite her colleague(s) to speak on their own behalf.
- *Giving the people on the buyer's side the opportunity to introduce themselves* by saying who they are, their

positions and responsibilities, and what would make the meeting a success from their perspectives.

- *Stating or reiterating the time* that has been agreed upon for the meeting, and checking that the buyer agrees to commit this amount of time. This matters, because if someone needs to leave early, it's better to know up front!

The role of the sales professional/meeting facilitator is to also manage the transitions during the meeting, whether it is the shift from rapport building to reviewing the agenda, or from presenting an insight to discussing the client's business needs, for example.

Presence Characteristics, Traits, and Behaviors during the Opening Phase

- comfort in your own skin
- awareness of self and others
- projection of a sense of ease, poise, or self-assurance,
- relaxed alertness
- communication of values and beliefs

Allows you to:
- show vulnerability
- connect
- engage
- build meaningful relationships
- establish credibility

2. Exploration/Discovery Phase

The second phase of a typical sales process is about exploration and discovery. In the traditional consultative selling process, the sales professional asks questions to learn as much as possible about the client's needs. During this phase, it's about putting yourself into the role of curious interviewer, taking the time to formulate and ask a range of questions that will help to uncover as much information as you can related to the client and their particular situation.

Richardson, a US-based sales-training organization, points out that buyers now are more informed and have higher expectations and increasing demands on the sales professionals who call on them. It is no longer enough to just show up with a pad and pen in hand and ask questions that you hope will help you uncover a business opportunity. Sometimes such a conversation needs to be preempted by the sales professional bringing an insight or idea to the buyer to get his or her attention. As Richardson points out in their white paper, "Selling with Insights," "these insights or ideas at the right time and in the right way can truly help a sales professional to differentiate themselves, drive business outcome-based discussions, and create a sense of urgency in the buyer."[5] I discuss presenting insights in more detail in chapter 3.

This phase is not just about discovering the buyer's needs; it's also about discovering or more aptly *qualifying* whether they are a fit for what you are selling.

The way to get to this decision point is through questioning. You are seeking to uncover your buyers' needs or pain points, against which you can position your product or service as the ideal solution.

If the objective is to learn in more detail what the buyer is trying to accomplish, then the sales professional's task is to ask buyers questions to understand as fully as possible what problems they are trying to address, issues they are trying to resolve, or opportunities they are trying to pursue, for example. Information is power, and the more information you have, the better able you are to align what you sell with what the buyer is trying to accomplish. So, it's not a choice between insight selling or consultative selling, nowadays sales professionals need to be able to embrace either approach contingent on the buyer situation or the perceived opportunity.

The reality often is that sales professionals don't spend enough time making inquiries about what ails their buyers *before* presenting a recommendation. It's not just about asking the right number of questions. More importantly, it's about asking the *right kind* of questions in the right way. These are questions that get beneath the surface of an initial response from the buyer, that go beyond learning a piece of data, or are thought provoking.

Whether you are meeting with a buyer to learn more about an opportunity or you have preempted a discussion by bringing an insight or offering an idea, you need to be prepared to orient the conversation toward learning about the buyer's thoughts, reactions, hopes, desires, needs, or pain points.

A sample of the kinds of questions sales-training companies teach include the following:

What do you make of _____?
How do you feel about _____?
What concerns you the most about _____?
What do you think about doing _____ this way?
What would prevent you from doing _____?
Why do you feel _____ is important?
What do you mean by _____?
What are the biggest issues facing your business/industry, in your view?
Tell me more about _____.
What else?
How can I/my team be most helpful to you?

What is your ideal outcome?

What else do you need to consider?

What are your next steps?

Note that the above examples are all what are called open-ended questions or questions that invite the buyer to offer his or her objective or subjective views and opinions.

Other specific details need to be learned through asking more pointed or closed-ended questions, such as the following:

- How long has _____ been a problem?
- What's your ideal cost/investment/budget?
- By when would you like to make a decision?
- Who is involved in the decision?
- What locations will be affected?

Ultimately, your goal is to paint as detailed a picture as you can about the buyer's business, personal, short-term, and long-term needs. This will help you understand the viability of the opportunity and how you can most persuasively present yourself, your team, your solution, and organization as the absolute right choice for the buyer.

Presence Characteristics, Traits, and Behaviors During the Exploration Phase

- empathy
- listening
- making good eye contact
- awareness of self and others
- genuine curiosity to know and understand

Allows you to:

- be trusted
- facilitate
- collaborate
- be creative
- speak truth to power

3. **Presentation Phase**

Traditionally in the typical sales process, having completed a sufficient exploration or following a discussion provoked by an insight presentation, the sales professional now has the opportunity to present a recommendation to the buyer. It requires taking what has been learned about the buyer's situation and persuasively presenting what you offer as the ideal or right solution as a means to solve the buyer's needs related to a problem or opportunity.

Depending on the complexity of the sale, a presentation can range from minutes or hours, to a presentation that evolves as new information surfaces and the buyer provides feedback.

Some key components of a successful presentation include the following:

- aligns with the buyer's needs
- demonstrates value to the buyer of the seller's product or solution
- is persuasive
- is engaging and interactive
- invites feedback

Presence Characteristics, Traits, and Behaviors During the Presentation Phase

- congruency of voice, body, and content
- authenticity
- confidence
- passion
- boldness
- expressiveness

Allows you to:

- inspire
- put your best foot forward
- influence
- be trusted

Sales presentations will be discussed in detail in chapter 3.

4. **Manage Resistance Phase**

This phase of the sales process is associated with managing the client's resistance to what you have presented as the solution. Resistance can come in many forms. It may be related to any number of things, including misunderstanding or confusion, dissatisfaction with the terms, timing, or perceived value of the offering. Whatever the reason or motivation, managing the buyer's resistance relates to facilitating a conversation with the intention of navigating a way toward a successful outcome for both parties.

Some of the things buyers say:

"Leave it with me, and I'll think about it."
"I'm not sure my boss/the committee will agree to this."
"The price is more than I expected."
"This won't work right now."
"We've decided to move in a different direction."

Some of the things buyers do:

- don't make a decision
- look or sound bored, frustrated, impatient
- stop paying attention and focus on their electronic devices
- stop returning e-mails and calls

Resistance can happen at any point in the sales cycle. Whether it's reluctance to engage in an open conversation, an unwillingness to respond to communications from the sales professional, or an explicit expression of opposition to what is being discussed or presented, resistance can trigger sales professionals to behave in a way that can cause us not to be our best, most present selves! Managing resistance is discussed in more detail in chapter 4.

A senior technology consultant and team leader, let's call him Jack, told me a story about trying to sell his organization's services to a global technology company. The technology company had decided to make a paradigm shift in the way they conducted their business. They were talking to the senior consultant and his team about engaging their organization as one of two providers. They would be a critical component in the successful implementation of the new strategy. Over the course of two years, many discussions and presentations had taken place. The consultant team was at the prospect's headquarters yet again, and had just completed an updated presentation. The usual conversation ensued. The senior consultant fearing that stasis would continue decided to intervene. He turned to the executive charged with making the final decision, let's call him Jeff, and asked with genuine curiosity "Jeff, would you be willing to talk about what is preventing you, personally, from making a decision to move forward with our organization?"

With that the executive stood up from the table, turned his back on the meeting attendees and looked out the window for several minutes. Jack recounted to me that he was getting repeated worried glares and quizzical glances from his teammates until Jeff finally turned to face the meeting again. He politely asked everyone to leave except Jack. In the conversation that ensued, Jeff told Jack his fears about the impact of a failed implementation not just on the organization, but also on his career. "I'll lose my job if we don't deliver" he said at one point. With this on the table, they discussed ways to make sure they engaged the right people from Jack's team, ran pilots, and manage an implementation process that would not expose Jeff's organization to a catastrophic failure. They shook hands at the end of the conversation with clear next steps, finally moving the deal forward.

Presence Characteristics, Traits, and Behaviors During the Manage-Resistance Phase

- breathing
- empathy
- listening
- awareness of self and others
- curiosity to know and understand

Allows you to:

- be flexible
- recover more quickly
- read the audience and adjust

5. Close Phase

In a well-managed consultative sales process, getting to a successful close becomes a natural outcome of dealing with the buyer's resistance, objections or pushback and successfully negotiating any aspect of the deal that requires such attention.

There are many ways to get there: the buyer says he or she wants to get started, the sales professional asks for the business, or the phone call or e-mail arrives with an affirmative answer after an arduous decision-making process among a multitude of buyer stakeholders.

Closing the deal is the "ring the bell" moment for a sales professional. It relates to all the practical and legal things that have to happen to get the paperwork signed and the implementation underway once the buyer has said yes.

Today's buyers are too sophisticated and informed to respond to manipulative phrases such as "If we could find a way to deal with [objection], would you sign the contract on [set period in time]?" or "Is there any reason, if we gave you the product at this price, that you wouldn't do business with our company?"

Our work includes using our presence effectively throughout the sales cycle, negating the need to use tricks or overly manipulative behavior to close the deal.

Presence Characteristics, Traits, and Behaviors During the Close Phase

- confidence
- awareness of self and others
- attentiveness
- Flexibility

Allows you to:

- collaborate
- influence
- be trusted

For many years I focused on improving my use of a sales process. There's no doubt it helped me increase my close ratio. The realization of what, from a presence perspective, I wasn't bringing to my sales efforts came after I participated in an improvisation theater workshop. So began my work on my presence as a sales professional. The good news is the work has made a marked improvement in my performance. The bad news is the work is ongoing!

CHAPTER 3

In this chapter I will:

◆ Illustrate the importance of presence during a presentation

◆ Summarize the behaviors and skills related to a presentation process

◆ Discuss and apply the ideal presence behaviors and skills during each component of the presentation

◆ Offer a structure for telling impactful stories

◆ Identify typical presence spoilers

◆ Detail exercises to improve your presence

PRESENTATIONS: PROCESS AND PRESENCE

Arguably, sales-training companies have focused on teaching a sales process rather than selling presence because the former is helpful to salespeople *and* its use is relatively easy to measure: Did you state the agenda? How many open-ended questions did you ask? What features and benefits did you highlight? However, giving feedback to a person about his or her presence is more subjective and requires greater sensitivity. How you made a group of buyers feel about your team, your organization, and your product is much more subjective than, say, making sure to emphasize the three main financial benefits while the CFO was in the room. Perhaps that's why our presence as sales professionals doesn't get the attention it deserves and needs. Yet, in a commoditized world where little if any product differentiation exists for any length of time, *you* are often the difference in whether the buyer chooses your solution or your competitor's.

What follows is a short story to illustrate the more challenging aspects of a large-group presentation. It happened to me, and it wasn't a whole lot of fun.

"And finally, I want to introduce you all to the latest member of our team. Joining our team, having moved here from Ireland, is Reggie Pearse." The crowd managed the kind of lame applause usually heard around two in the morning at an open-mic standup-comedy club. I inhaled a deep breath into a rapidly seizing chest cavity.

"Reggie has promised me he'd entertain you with a good horseracing joke and also give you an overview of our current crop of investment opportunities." The crowd fell silent.

I froze in fear with a smile stuck to my face, as this was the first presentation I'd made in front of a large American audience. I did an internal scan. I'd stopped breathing. Bad sign! Then I noticed my brain telling me that flight was not an option: new career; large, mostly attentive audience; and a half dozen tables between me and the exit. I would stay and do my best.

As I began to stand, my tie dragged across the dessert bowl through a mixture of fruit juice and cream. I continued rising as if completing the second half of a bow, and discreetly wiped my tie with a napkin. Successfully executing this maneuver gave me a jolt of self-confidence. With my senses on high alert,

I made decisions in rapid-fire succession: don't bother with pleasantries, here's an introduction to the joke, go. I was having an out-of-body experience of sorts. I began, "A version of the story I'm going to tell you has been going around amongst the punters at race tracks and beyond for many years. It was told to me by a good friend of mine, the jockey in the story, Paddy Barnes.

Paddy has just been given a new mount by his employer, the trainer Vincent O'Donnell. He takes the horse out for a gallop and quickly realizes that this three year old by the renowned stallion Seattle Slew is something special. Something very special, as he recalled to me at the time. The gelding covered ground with an ease and self-confidence Paddy hadn't experienced in a long time.

A few months later Paddy is chosen to ride this gifted mount in his maiden race. As he's about to be given a leg up Vincent leans into Paddy and says, "Bring him home in third or fourth, no higher ya hear? Let's save him for another day."

The race goes off and Paddy's horse is a little slow out of the gate but quickly catches the other horses tucking himself in along the rail in the middle of the field of seven. The first time past the stand in the 10 furlong race, you could have thrown a blanket over six of the field they were so tightly bunched. A single straggler was just falling off the pace. Paddy keeps the horse in fourth through the lower turn and back stretch. As they approach the three furlong marker the leading horse makes his move and is followed quickly by the second and third horse. Paddy, determined to follow orders, delays urging the horse on by a couple of seconds – just long enough to leave some daylight between him and the others ahead. In the final stretch Paddy goes to work with enough vigor to hold his fourth place managing to cross the finish with an accelerating horse. "Moved late" would be the handicapper's comment.

"Well?" said Vincent as Paddy dismounted.

"I'll tell you one thing for sure, I'd have easily beaten those three horses ahead of me." was Paddy's confident initial report.

"That's great news!" says Vincent.

"It is. Though the thing is I can't say for sure I would've beaten the three that finished behind me."

There's a moments silence as neurons fire in my audience's brains and then an uproarious laughter catches on like wildfire. They loved it. My confidence soared as I began to present our investment opportunities.

I tell this story, but not necessarily the tepid joke, because it represents one extreme of what can happen internally to sales professionals in the moments before a big presentation to a group: the increase in anxiety resulting in shallow breathing, sweaty palms, and flight impulses.

For some sales professionals, presenting is their moment of glory. They get to shine in the spotlight and talk about their insight, products or services. For others, particularly when presenting to groups, there is some degree of anxiety attached to making the presentation or pitch.

Of course, not all sales presentations are to a group of buyers. One-on-one sales presentations are more easily managed interactions. That said, if the stakes are high, the pressure to succeed can certainly provoke some anxiety! Whatever the size of your audience, there are universally applicable skills and behaviors that will help increase the impact of your presentations. I will begin with the ideal process-related skills and behaviors and then focus on presence.

BEHAVIORS AND SKILLS FOR PRESENTATIONS: PROCESS

Make time to set up. If the buyer allows, arrive early to the room in which you'll be presenting. Give yourself enough time before the presentation to set up your equipment, product samples, and any other props you'll be using.

Being able to make sure technology is working properly and seating arrangements are optimal, and getting a feel for the space in general before the buyer arrives can have a calming effect on jangly nerves.

However, not all situations will allow for such a luxury. The alternative is to set up in the buyer's presence. Doing so with calm and poise, and sometimes making it a collaborative effort, can serve to create a rapport and connection before the formal presentation begins, unlike the experience recounted in the story in chapter 1, where a poorly managed setup damaged, rather than enhanced, credibility. Remember, your presentation in terms of how you convey who you are and your presence as an individual or presenting team begins the moment the buyer sets eyes on you.

Open the meeting. As discussed in the previous chapter, a sales presentation should begin with introductions, a review of the agenda, and the time contract.

Review the buyer's needs, goals, and objectives. A formal presentation is usually, though not always, a culmination of a series of meetings and discussions with the buyer. It's often the result of a series of conversations where business and/or personal needs, problems, and opportunities were discussed.

Ideally, every sales presentation should begin in this way. The benefits include the following:

- It ensures everyone at the meeting is coalescing around the same set of buyer needs and objectives.
- It brings meeting attendees who may not have been involved in earlier interactions up to speed.
- It allows the presenters to tie the benefits of their recommended solution directly to the agreed-upon needs of the buyer.

Presenting Insights. According to Richardson,

The use of insights at the right time and in the right way can truly help a seller to differentiate themselves, drive business outcome-based discussions, and create a sense of urgency in the buyer. Sellers can do this by encouraging customers to think about their business issues and needs in a new way. This includes helping the customer to get past their own misunderstandings and misperceptions in order to make the best decisions for the business. Sellers must bring relevant insights and ideas to create value in the buying experience itself rather than just in the solution that the seller delivers.[1]

Insights are used to

1. be thought provoking by sometimes introducing paradigm-shifting opinions or beliefs
2. educate the buyer on new ideas and opportunities
3. create the opportunity to collaborate and problem solve with the buyer
4. create a business opportunity for both parties

Presenting Insights and making recommendations.
When presenting an insight or proposing a solution,
you should do the following:

1. Ensure it is relevant to your buyer. See the
previous point about reviewing your buyer's needs at
the beginning of your presentation. The core of your
presentation should focus on how your insight, product
or solution addresses the conscious and/or unconscious
needs of the buyer.

2. Have a vertical takeoff. Get to the key impacts
or opportunities of your insight, or the benefits of
your product or solution to the buyer early in the
presentation. The benefit in this context is the benefit
to the buyer of reacting to the insight or the value
your product or solution will bring to your buyers
in relation to their needs or pain points, challenges
or opportunities. There is no point in having a forty-
slide deck if the most relevant slides to the problems
your buyer is trying to solve are near the back of the
deck. They'll likely have switched off long before you
get there! This means your presentation should be
customized to relate to that which is most important
to your buyer.

*3. Tell stories that use data to support your key
points.* If a picture is worth a thousand words, then
a well-told, relevant story is worth a thousand data
points in a sales presentation. According to *Harvard
Business Review,* a data-driven presentation is now a
crucial skill for many professionals, since we often have
to tell our colleagues a story about the success of a new
initiative, the promise of a new business opportunity,
or the imperative of a change in strategy—stories that
are much more compelling when they're backed by
numbers.[2]

However, it is important to use it sparingly. Data should
support your story rather than become a distraction

from your main messages. Don't bore your buyers with needless or irrelevant data. Suggestions on how to embed stories in a presentation is discussed in more detail in the presence section, below.

BEHAVIORS AND SKILLS FOR PRESENTATIONS: PRESENCE

The late, great sales guru and sales trainer David Sandler once said, "Selling is a Broadway play."[3] I believe he intended several things in this metaphor, including the notion that as sales professionals, we must be willing to fully embrace a role if we are to be successful.

To explore how we use our presence most effectively in a sales presentation, I am going to expand Sandler's use of the Broadway play metaphor by looking at the skills of an actor and reconciling them with the skills required of a sales professional making a presentation.

Consider this list of skills or characteristics of a successful actor:

Actor Skills
- authenticity
- vocal variety
- empathy
- clarity of purpose
- seeming relaxed
- self-confidence
- passion
- living in the moment
- breathing
- body language
- facial expression
- creativity
- emotional availability
- knowing your lines

- connecting with an audience
- flexibility
- rehearsal
- energy
- collaboration
- taking risks
- listening
- eye contact

We don't often think about acting skills when preparing a sales presentation. However, they are the same skills great sales presenters engage to make an effective presentation. Take a look at Figure 2 to review the application of actor/presence focus to a typical presentation. Later in the chapter, I will recommend exercises to improve these skills.

Presentation Process Component	Purpose	Acting skills/ Presence Focus
Planning	❑ be at your best on the day	❑ rehearsal ❑ collaboration ❑ taking risks ❑ creativity ❑ knowing your lines
Open the Meeting	❑ Introduction of participants ❑ Review of the agenda ❑ Confirm time contract	❑ authenticity ❑ empathy ❑ connecting with an audience ❑ seeming relaxed ❑ self-confidence

As relevant, review the buyer's strategy, needs, goals and objectives	Set a context for the presentation	❏ clarity of purpose ❏ flexibility
Present insight or make recommendation	As it relates to insights: ❏ be thought provoking ❏ educate the buyer on new ideas and opportunities, ❏ create the opportunity to collaborate and problem solve with the buyer ❏ create a business opportunity for both parties As it relates to recommendations: ❏ present the features and benefits of your recommendation to your buyer	❏ vocal variety ❏ breathing ❏ body language ❏ facial expression ❏ emotional availability ❏ listening ❏ eye contact ❏ living in the moment

Figure 2.

Telling stories. It has been my experience that we don't use stories frequently enough in formal sales presentations. We tend to lean on data and facts as a means to persuade. Yet the evidence shows that stories are more persuasive. Here are some tips for how to craft an effective business-related story in your sales presentation. Your story will be relevant if you use the following structure:

- *Start with a business context.* "Our customer service score has improved by _____ percent"
- *Tell the story.* "How this trend began was last year we ..."
- *Say what you learned from the story.* "We heard loud and clear ..."
- *Translate what it means to this buyer.* "What this means to you ..."

Your story will be well told if you use the following techniques:

- *Create emotional resonance.* Tell a story that will resonate at an emotional level with your audience.
- *Use simple language.* Rather than long, descriptive sentences, use concise language that lets your buyer draw conclusions.
- *Use your body, face, and voice.* Your body is a 3-D picture. Use it instead of words.

Finally, make your presentation interactive. Just because you have been invited to present to a buyer or earned the right to do so does not mean that your presentation should be a monologue. Check in with your buying audience as you move through the presentation, seeking their reaction and feedback. Most complex sales are an iterative process, so hearing constructive feedback early will make the meeting more engaging and productive for you and your buyer.

IMPROVING YOUR PRESENCE

There is an old joke among sales professionals that the hope is always to have a meeting with a buyer take place on the top floor of a high-rise office building. This allows the sales team enough time, while riding up in the elevator, to plan how they will run the meeting. It is a somewhat amusing image and, unfortunately, in reality an inadequate planning huddle that happens all too often. Anecdotal evidence abounds of sales professionals showing up to presentations armed with the usual slide deck and a lot of hope.

Athletes spend most of their time practicing, and actors spend much of their time rehearsing, but for some reason, many of us in selling adopt an "it'll be all right on the night" approach. With this approach, we run the risk of being triggered into manifesting any of the presence spoilers listed below. I think we have something to learn from athletes and actors! Winning margins are often tight when winning a sale. Using a traditional sales process could possibly differentiate you from some of your competitors. A great presence in a commoditized world can be the winning margin.

The first step in developing or improving a skill is becoming conscious of the change(s) you need to make. Once you have decided to work on something, you must keep it in mind by bringing conscious attention to the change as often as you can. David Rock and Jeffrey Schwartz, in their article "The Neuroscience of Leadership," coined the term "attention density."[4] For change to actually take place and stick, they say we must bring our attention to it frequently and consciously. Therefore, it is best to work on developing or improving one skill or competency at a time.

Consider the list of typical presence spoilers:

- pacing the floor or fidgeting
- speaking too quickly
- speaking in a higher register
- Upspeak (when the tone of your voice goes up at the end of a sentence)
- running out of breath before the end of a sentence

- keeping poor eye contact with the buyer
- not listening to the buyer or not observing and responding appropriately to the buyer's nonverbal reactions

Presenters who manifest these behaviors are experiencing classic fight-or-flight symptoms, where heightened anxiety levels can cause us to struggle to contain the increase in cortisol and adrenaline in our bodies. This energy tends to leak out and show up in the ways I have listed above.

We have the greatest possibility of showing up with relaxed alertness if we have spent time in rehearsal. According to Daniel Goleman, "A relaxed mind is a productive mind."[5]

Effective sales presenters are good at seeming relaxed. It's the "duck swimming across water" metaphor: looking calm and poised above the water, while beneath the surface its legs and feet are working at a furious pace. For some, we can't even fake it. The ideal is to achieve a place of calm, both internally and externally. Having internal calm allows us to project a sense of ease, poise, and self-assurance while experiencing relaxed alertness. For some of us, the best we can do is learn how to appear relaxed.

Continuing the acting metaphor, one of the great actor-training methodologies is one created and used by the late Constantin Stanislavski, the renowned Russian stage actor and director. A quote attributed to him says, "Rehearsal is the anxiety, performance the relaxation."[6] His intention in saying this to actors was to encourage them to work through their performance anxiety during a repeated rehearsal process. The familiarity they had with the role and material by the time the curtain went up or the camera rolled allowed them to be fully present.

I believe sales professionals involved in team selling could benefit from the Stanislavski approach particularly. Getting the "who's going to say what," the transitions and continuity, and importantly, the chemistry right adds exponentially to a team presentation.

The place to begin improving your presentation presence is with an understanding of what's working for you and what isn't. Ideally, you should get feedback from someone whose opinion you respect and who has seen you give presentations. This is someone who will be candid and specific about your presence.

Read Your Buyer Audience and Respond Appropriately

Have you ever had a great first meeting—you connected well, conversation flowed easily, and you came away with solid next steps—only to return to make a presentation and it feels like something or someone sucked the air out of the room, making you question your conclusion that the first meeting had put you on a solid footing? These are the moments that test our ability to stay present when confronted with unanticipated buyer behavior. In these situations making the planned for presentation without trying to understand the changed dynamic is likely to be an unproductive choice.

As I said earlier, we need to tune in to our buyer audience at the macro and micro levels. With this in mind, imagine a meeting on a Friday afternoon. The buyer team is in the middle of a new vendor-selection process. You are the sixth presentation they've sat through that particular day. Chances are, they will not be struggling to contain their enthusiasm! On the contrary, the most noteworthy initial experience you have is their jaded, though mildly polite, demeanor.

So, the question to ask yourself is *what do I need to do?* One option is doing what you always do in the same way you've always done it—agenda, introductions, discovery, presentation,

Q and A, next steps—perhaps you let their energy dictate the overall energy of the meeting.

An alternative and more effective option is to meet your buyers where they are. This is about using your social awareness to be cognizant of the mood, needs, time of day, and what's going on for them emotionally and physiologically. Put yourself in their shoes and think how you'd feel if you were about to begin your sixth meeting on the same topic. Not great, I'd bet! The second part is to use your presence to lift their level of energy and engagement to gain their attention.

EXERCISES TO IMPROVE YOUR PRESENCE

Goal: *Using breath to relax.* Project a sense of ease, poise, and self-assurance, helping to connect with, engage, and inspire your audience.

As mentioned in chapter 1, breathing is an often-quoted means for calming oneself, to the point that it can be dismissed along the lines of "Well, I know about breathing, but isn't there anything else?" The answer is, with the exception of taking medication, there is no other way we can directly affect our autonomic nervous system. Think about it; you can't directly control your heart rate, perspiration, or the release of cortisol and adrenaline (fight-or-flight hormones). However, we can indirectly, through breathing. A long inhaled breath and a slightly longer exhaled breath for several minutes sends a message to the brain to slow the heart, calming the nervous system.

Exercise: Practice deep breathing
To practice deep breathing, inhale through your nose and exhale through your mouth. Remember to do the following:

- breathe more slowly
- breathe more deeply, from the belly
- exhale longer than you inhale

Try the following: take a breath into your belly (i.e., expanding your diaphragm) to the count of six, pause for a second, and then breathe out slowly through a small hole in your mouth to a count of seven. Exhaling through your mouth instead of your nose makes your breathing a conscious process, not a subconscious one. If you own a Fitbit or the Apple watch you have a readily available tool to help you with this exercise.

The oxygen supply to your body's cells increases, and this helps produce endorphins, the body's feel-good hormones. A consequence of this is that your muscles will relax, including, importantly, your facial muscles.

Goal: *Improve eye contact.* Enhance credibility, be more emotionally available, and connect with your buyer audience.

Presenters avoid making eye contact for many reasons, including fear that eye contact will increase nervousness, a lack of preparation or comfort with the content, or wanting to avoid coming on too strong by looking directly at the audience, or just habitually looking away from the other. Whatever your reason, and whether you look up, down, or your eyes dart about the room, not holding eye contact long enough for the buyer to feel connected to you makes you seem less confident, lacking in authority, and therefore less believable. With some practice, this is a very fixable behavior.

Exercise: Eye-Contact Coaching

Tell a few people you trust that you are working on the skill of improving your level of eye contact—specifically that you want to avoid always looking away while talking. They will be your coaches. On your instructions, during conversations with you, tell them to raise their hand to signal to you when they feel connected through eye contact. Your work is not to learn to hold a hard stare when talking but to look someone in the eye long enough to *see* them and *be seen by them*. Your coach will be the judge! Yes, it's going to feel immensely awkward at first, so allow enough time, likely several months, to work through the discomfort and setbacks as you seek to develop and internalize the new behavior.

Goal: *Convey confidence.* Body, voice, face, and emotion should all be working together to help communicate your message more powerfully and persuasively.

"What you do speaks so loudly, I can't hear what you're saying." was noted by Ralph Waldo Emerson and it is still true today.

This emphasizes the importance of congruence of body, voice, face, and emotion when communicating a message. Look at the following example:

> *Sales professional (verbal):* I feel really excited to tell you that our solution will meet everything you're trying to accomplish.

> *Sales professional (nonverbal):* Avoids eye contact, looks anxious, has a closed body language, etc.

> The most likely interpretation is that the sales professional does not fully embrace what he is saying as being true.

Congruency in body, voice, face, and emotion is not an accident. It is the result of thousands of years of evolution. We humans are pack animals, and as such, we need to communicate to each other quickly and decisively. Most particularly this system of communication—the body, voice, and face—conveying emotions, has evolved to help keep us safe. Paul Eckman, most recently, has done fascinating research on how our emotions have evolved and how they serve to help us make decisions. His work has found that for most of us, our work is to become conscious of our emotions *before* we speak or act. Again, for most of us, that's really difficult.[7]

The importance of having an emotional appeal has been highlighted by the work of Stephen Porges as well. His research has shown that, physiologically, our bodies evolved to expect co-regulation and reciprocity from others. The absence of danger in an environment doesn't make people feel safe. It's receiving cues from others that triggers our sense of safety. Having a strong social engagement system, that includes lots of safety cues, is how we grow and develop and acquire resilience.[8]

In a selling context, Porges's work suggests that congruency of message and body language says, "Mr. Buyer, you will be safe should you choose to work with us."

I.   **Exercise (with Partner): Jump Emotions**
      The best exercise I know for practicing congruency of expression brings us to improvisational theater and more particularly to an activity called Jump Emotions.[9] You can do this activity with a partner. My wife, who was in an improv comedy troupe in the late 80's taught me this activity, which was how her troupe auditioned new players. Your partner gives you a topic on which to speak, Something noncontroversial works well, for example, travel, weather, or decorating. Then your partner calls out different emotions, for example anger, love, disgust, excitement, fear, pride, surprise, embarrassment, sadness, and joy. While speaking as if you are an expert, your main goal is to convey the given emotion at a high intensity. You are trying to

allow your body, voice, and face to convey the emotion, even more than your words. Your coach changes the emotion every fifteen or twenty seconds, giving you an opportunity to shift and feel the dramatic difference in your physicality in each of the emotions. Tell your partner to change the emotions five or six times. Notice how your tone shifts, and notice the change in your energy and your facial expressions.

Ask your partner for some feedback about what she sees as strengths and areas for development in your capacity to express emotions congruently, because it is so easy to shut someone down when they are trying to behave in ways that are not habitual. The most important thing your partner can do is to provide a supportive and encouraging environment, because safety is probably the single most important ingredient for anyone to be able to stretch his or her comfort zone in congruency.

Now it is your turn. Switch roles. You can learn as much from watching your partner. Give your partner a topic. When you call out the emotions, see if you can express the emotions on your face as well while your partner is taking his or her turn. You should be warmed up and ready to show emotions from the last round. Encourage your partner by showing him or her what the emotions look like on your face. Like your partner did for you, change the emotions every 15-20 seconds and about five or six times. Now you give feedback, and remember to give lots of positive feedback to encourage safety.

Notice how you feel after this exercise. I imagine you will notice a little more relaxation and calm and openness. Something wonderful happens to the nervous systems of most of us when we allow ourselves to express in a more dramatic way. It seems to free something when we allow our bodies to return to their most natural and primitive form of communication. The body holds no secrets.

II.   **Exercise: The Power Pose**

Amy Cuddy, a social psychologist at Harvard University, published a popular work demonstrating that two minutes of "power poses" a day can change our body chemistry. Increased levels of testosterone and decreased levels of cortisol, the stress hormone in the brain, affect not only the sense of power we feel but also the confidence we convey.

Cuddy describes poses demonstrating power as ones where the individual "takes up [physical] space" or "[becomes] big." An example of this is the Wonder Woman pose.[10] Though I can't imagine too many in our profession striking such a pose as we wait for the meeting to begin! However, Cuddy suggests using a bathroom stall or other private space as a practical venue in which to strike the pose. We need to pay attention to is our posture, avoiding rounded shoulders and eyes cast downward, which Cuddy's research says is disempowering.

Power pose

Link to Amy Cuddy Ted Talk:
https://www.ted.com/ talks/amy_cuddy_your_body_language_
shapes_who_you_are?language=en

Goal: *Become more flexible and spontaneous.* People who are able to think on their feet are more comfortable in their skin.

Daniel Pink, in his book *To Sell Is Human*, encourages anyone involved in selling to take an improvisational acting class.[11] He's right! The benefits can be profound. You will learn to trust yourself more in the moment, which will allow you to be more flexible and adaptive during client interactions. Jump Emotions is a great tool for getting better at thinking on your feet as well as the congruency we discussed above. Being a good improviser means being a good listener. In improv training, you learn to pay attention, to be in the moment, and to focus on your partner's every word. You learn to pay attention to all his or her body-language cues, and you learn to build positively on what has come before.

While improvisational techniques are often used extensively in drama programs to train actors, the skills and processes of improvisation are also used outside the context of performing arts as a way to develop communication skills.

Improv theater activities such as the ones listed below can help sales professionals improve the discipline of listening fully before responding. It also enhances your ability to trust yourself to respond positively and creatively in the moment. Most sales professionals balk at the suggestion of taking an improvisational theater class. Their calendars are suddenly chock full of trips and meetings. I get it. It's challenging work. I can personally vouch for the benefits of completing an improv theater session, or better still, a few sessions.

Exercises: Improv theater activities

1. **Yes, And (with partner)...**

This activity teaches us how to listen, accept what is being said, and build on what we have heard. This is an excellent skill set to have when you are problem solving or brainstorming with buyers. In the game of "Yes, And ..." you will learn the skill of saying yes to whatever is offered. You are required to accept your partner's ideas and build on them. For example, at the beginning of the scene, character number one will begin by establishing setting and plot:

Character #1: What a hot and miserable day to be a ranch hand!

(Following the "Yes, And ..." method, character number two will accept the premise and add on to the situation.)

Character #2: Yes, and the boss said we gotta count every last head of cattle before the day ends.

(The scene continues with each partner starting his lines with "yes, and ...")

Character #1: Yes, and isn't it easy for him to say that while he sits in the shade all day?

2. **Story, Story, Die (with a Group)**

This is an excellent group exercise to improve listening skills and improve your ability to trust your instincts and creativity. This activity requires between three and five storytellers and one facilitator.

Storytellers form a line. The facilitator gives a title for a story and a story genre and begins the activity by pointing to a participant, who needs to start telling the story. The facilitator then points at different storytellers, who need to continue the story flawlessly, even if the switch has happened in the middle of a sentence or even in the middle of a word.

Storytellers who hesitate or whose sentences are not grammatically correct or don't make sense, are pronounced "dead" by the facilitator (which means the storyteller must fall down or out of line). The last participant left standing in line ends the story.

Embedded in all the exercises above are some important principles of improv theater that also apply to sales presence:

- Make everyone else look good (your buyer and teammates).
- There are no mistakes, only opportunities to recover and adjust. (a useful orientation when sales calls don't go well).
- Listen, listen, listen.

There are a range of improv theater exercises available at http://spolingamesonline.org/games/.

Making time to work on our presence is easy to put on the long finger. It does take time, progress is not necessarily linear, and it's hard to measure. All I can do is advocate for the value of building it into your development plan. If you're willing to immerse yourself in it from time to time, be open to the outcomes, and take some risks, the payback will come. Some of the skill-building activities I highlighted are a heck of a lot of fun.

CHAPTER 4

In this chapter I will:

◆ Offer an example of effective meeting management

◆ Discuss the impact of having the 'right' presence when managing meetings with buyers

◆ Identify the tasks and skills of a sales professional in a facilitator role

◆ Present the ideal facilitator presence by meeting type including:

        o   discovery meeting
        o   presentation meeting
        o   conflict resolution meeting
        o   problem-solving meeting

MEETING MANAGEMENT

In the introduction to the book I mentioned that CEB reported our buyers believe we sales professionals are not evolving our skills quickly enough to align with changing buyer behavior. One way we can develop our skillset is to become more effective meeting facilitators. What follows is a fable of a problem-solving meeting.

"Good morning, everybody. It's great to see you all here together. Carla, I know you fought hard against the New York traffic to get here on time. And, Bill, I know your travel schedule is particularly crazy this week. Thank you all for making it.

The purpose of the meeting, as you've seen in the correspondence in the run up to today, is to discuss the changes in your respective industries and businesses and to share ideas on what you will need from an organization like ours into the future.

Before I share a detailed agenda, let's do a round of introductions. Then, before we dig into the content, I'll get everyone out of his or her seat for a brief icebreaker."

That's how the four-hour problem-solving session began with eight buyers from a variety of industries, ably hosted and facilitated by Selena Mendez, the number-one sales professional for Ariat Technologies Corporation for the third year in a row.

The meeting started at 9:00 a.m., and by 9:20 a.m., Selena had her buyers—some relatively new and others having worked with her for three or more years—out of their seats, laughing their way through a light physical icebreaker. When the group sat down to dig into the first agenda item, the energy was high. The attendees were engaged and connected as though they had known each other for a long time.

The meeting was a mixture of group and paired discussions, idea generation, debate, and sharing of best practices. By the time they broke for lunch, Selena and her team had a large whiteboard filled with suggestions, ideas, and requests for how she and her organization could help her buyers survive and thrive in the rapidly changing business environment ("helter-skelter," as one participant called his organization's business environment).

When debriefing after the meeting, Selena said she was struck by how hungry her buyers were to hear how their peers were addressing similar challenges. The ways in which they helped each other were an unintended consequence of the meeting, she concluded.

Patrick Lencioni, in his book titled *Death by Meeting*, says that "Meetings are a puzzling paradox. On one hand, they are critical ... on the other hand, they are painful. Frustratingly long and seemingly pointless."[1]

Most meetings between a sales professional and a buyer suffer a similar fate. All too often, buyers don't share the excitement a sales professional feels once the meeting is arranged. To excel as a sales professional and to differentiate yourself from your competitors, you need to become an effective meeting planner, designer, and facilitator. The goal is to be the sales professional with whom your buyers look forward to spending time because they know the meeting will be a purposeful, engaging, creative, and productive encounter.

YOUR PRESENCE AND MEETING MANAGEMENT

As the meeting facilitator, you are in a powerful position to create a meeting dynamic that is, as described earlier in the book, psychologically safe. It's a dynamic that, ideally, inspires collaboration and openness—a transparent exchange of opinions, ideas, hopes, and fears. Of course, on reading this, your mind immediately goes to your most difficult and demanding buyer, and you think, *yeah, right*. Maybe for those buyers, it's the more difficult challenge of shifting a preexisting bad dynamic. It's not impossible, just harder than starting a new relationship or improving one that is okay.

It is through your presence that you manifest this power and influence. When meeting attendees sense a genuine interest on your part to engage in a meaningful way, to take care of them by respecting their time and input, and to respond with understanding and flexibility to what evolves during the meeting, they in turn are more likely to respond in a positive and productive way.

To understand the importance of the right presence in this role, let's first look at what effective meeting facilitators do.

Before the meeting, they do the following:

- define the purpose of the meeting and create and circulate the agenda
- ensure the right people are invited
- coordinate logistics, including time, location, equipment, and refreshments

During the meeting, they do the following:

- create a warm and friendly atmosphere
- are interested and engaging
- manage time
- review the agenda and meeting objectives
- keep discussions on track
- ensure all voices are heard, particularly the buyer's
- remain aware of and responsive to the overall meeting and interpersonal dynamics as they evolve and shift; address those that could hurt the meeting objectives
- ask appropriate questions to stimulate conversation
- listen for what is being said and *not* said
- summarize the main points and reframe when necessary
- identify and coordinate next steps

So much of our success as the meeting facilitator is derived from the manner in which we show up in the role. It's about the genuine warmth with which we greet people, the sincere tone with which we ask questions, the disciplined way we stay attentive and listen, and the empathic way in which we stay connected to meeting attendees.

It can be the small things that make the difference as the facilitator. I was on a conference call recently with a prospective buyer. There were three of us on the seller side. Early in the call, the buyer said the key decision maker lived in Canada and rarely traveled to the United States. The call was going well. We were moving toward next steps when the meeting facilitator (the sales professional) said, "Why don't we all get together at your office in Boston?"

The buyer, with a hint of impatience, replied, "We can't, because she lives in Canada." We suffer small credibility wounds when we forget or don't listen to the details.

THE SALES PROFESSIONAL AS FACILITATOR

An outcome of a well-facilitated meeting is that the likelihood of surprises down the road from the buyer is reduced—it mitigates the possibility of hearing surprising objections such as "The timing is not right," "We don't have the budget for this," or "I need to get approval from HQ before we move forward."

It is the role of the facilitator to monitor the buyer's level of energy and engagement and be able to change the dynamic of the meeting based on those observations. The facilitator can do this with a verbal check-in about where their attention and thinking are. When this is done effectively, the success of the meeting becomes a shared responsibility of the buyer and the sales professional.

When in the role of facilitator, do the following well and consistently in live meetings, as you are the person to whom others will be looking for cues on how to behave:

Make Connections. Meet and greet meeting attendees. The goal is for people to feel included and valued, making it more likely for them to actively participate as the agenda items unfold. The right presence, one that exudes warmth, attentiveness, and empathy, is a key to creating the right atmosphere as people arrive and settle in.

Model and Encourage Behaviors. If your goal is to have a well-structured meeting with a clear agenda and desired outcomes, then your task at the outset is to communicate this.

- Have a hook in your opening to get participants' attention—something that tells "what's in it for me" from the buyer's perspective.
- Express your expectation about participation, and then encourage it by inviting attendees to offer an opinion, thought, or insight. The earlier in the meeting you can do this with your buyers, the more likely they are to engage actively throughout the meeting.
- Thank your buyers for their contribution, particularly early in the meeting.
- Encourage attendees to be candid, and when they offer a dissenting or contrary opinion, praise them.
- Pay attention to the level of participation on both sides, and adjust your facilitation based on the meeting structure and objective. For example, if the meeting structure is a presentation of an insight or idea, the facilitator needs to seek the buyer's feedback or reaction if it is not readily forthcoming.

- Be able to restate what someone said earlier in the meeting ("As Jack said earlier ..."), and tie it to the current discussion or ask for more detail.
- Summarize what has been expressed, check for understanding, and when necessary, reframe the content of the discussion as a problem to be solved or a need to be addressed.

Be Vulnerable. Vulnerability can be a challenging concept for some sales professionals to embrace. It certainly was for me! Our qualities of resilience and optimism, the ways of being that helped make us successful, can seem contrary to being vulnerable. However, vulnerability can be a powerful meeting climate setter. This idea is supported by research at the Harvard Negotiation Project. Their research demonstrated that the more we are willing to show vulnerability, the more likely it is the other person will reciprocate. [2]

Put simply, it can seem unfair if we as sellers only highlight all that we do well and then expect the buyers to reveal their challenges and weaknesses. A private wealth manager told me that he has built trust and grown relationships by telling his clients what he and his firm *don't* do well, meaning he has chosen to walk away from business opportunities because it was not in his client's best interests to work with his organization on that particular deal. While there is a short-term cost in the lost opportunity, there is added trust and credibility when he presents what they do well.

There are moments when vulnerability can set or change the tone of a meeting—responses such as these:

- I don't know the answer to that question, but I'd be happy to get it.
- That is something we don't do well.
- I get the sense I've lost you as an audience; is that right?

Whether big or small moments, the more sales professionals can model the way to having a "real" conversation, the quicker the buyer will get to "Yes," "No," or "What's next?".

Facilitating a virtual meeting is a bit more challenging than a meeting where everyone is physically present in the same room, because it is too easy for participants to get distracted by other things, such as e-mail and pressing tasks that need attention.

The same set of facilitation skills applies to virtual meetings as well, though with virtual meetings, the facilitator needs to more proactively do the following:

- Make sure the buyer is familiar with whatever technology and tools you are using.
- Help attendees connect with one another.
- Keep everyone engaged and away from distractions by calling on them by name. Keep an ear open for attendees from the buyer organization who are not participating.
- Summarize often and check for agreement and understanding.
- Be more rigorous in managing to the meeting process. For example, focus on one agenda item at a time. If the discussion goes in a couple of different directions at the same time, attendees are more likely to get confused or frustrated and check out.

Source: Edgework Consulting[3]

FACILITATION BY MEETING TYPE

In a sale with any degree of complexity, it is unlikely that the deal will be closed at the conclusion of the first meeting. Therefore, as you manage through the sales cycle with a prospective or existing buyer, different meetings will likely have different structures.

The meeting type will be determined by the purpose of the meeting. See Figure 3 for details. For example, at the beginning of a sales cycle in a discovery meeting, the focus is on the behaviors that will allow you to connect, engage, and establish trust and credibility. Later in the sales cycle, when presenting, the focus shifts to emphasizing behaviors that will influence, inspire and persuade.

Meeting Type	Purpose	Facilitator Presence
Discovery	Qualify and explore the scope of an opportunity with a prospect or existing buyer.	• Connect • Engage • Establish credibility • Show vulnerability
Presentation (Insight, Education, or Solution)	Offer a thought-provoking insight, educate the client on some aspect of the proposed solution, and present the value of your product or solution.	• Be passionate • Influence • Inspire • Persuade
Conflict Resolution	Resolve issue(s) that are preventing a buyer from agreeing to move forward with a deal, or address dissatisfaction in an existing relationship.	• Be curious • Be careful • Be courageous • Offer your contribution • Don't forget to breathe

Problem Solving	Collaborate with the buyer by pooling experience and expertise to identify creative or innovative solutions to challenging problems.	• Collaborate • Facilitate • Be flexible • Be creative

Figure 3.

Discovery Meeting

The classic consultative sales process emphasizes discovery of the buyer's needs as a precursor to presenting a solution. Facilitating a discovery meeting, as the title implies, means placing an emphasis on learning as much as you can about the buyer's situation. I have covered this process in some detail in chapter 2.

The analogy often used in explaining the intention and importance of the discovery meeting is that it is like a patient visiting the doctor's office, complaining of being unable to sleep. If the doctor were to respond only to that symptom, he or she may diagnose insomnia and prescribe a sleeping medication. However, if the doctor were to seek more information, he or she may discover that the patient's aching knee is what's keeping him from sleeping. It's an unlikely doctor-patient scenario but one that highlights the need, as a sales professional, to understand as much as you can about the buyer's "pain" before recommending a solution.

Conceptually, this makes sense, yet it is one of the most difficult facilitation skills for many sales professionals to manifest well and consistently, in my experience. To quote the late Steve Jobs of Apple "Get closer than ever to your customers. So close that you tell them what they need well before they realize it themselves." [4]

Most sales professionals will set out to facilitate a discovery meeting, aiming to ask questions and listen to their buyer's responses before recommending a solution. However—and this is where this type of meeting most often derails—the sales professional starts to present.

In a discovery meeting, focus on the following:

- creating psychological safety, through behaviors including taking time to connect with and engage your audience, and being vulnerable
- asking questions to understand
- reframing and summarizing what is said during the meeting
- avoiding the allure of presenting prematurely
- agreeing on next steps

Sales-Presentation Meetings

Sales presentations were discussed in detail in chapter 3.

Something to note in the context of meeting management and selling presence is what US-based sales-training organization Richardson says of presenting insights: "A key risk in leveraging insights is that the seller can easily come across as arrogant, manipulating, or self-serving if they aren't aware of and skilled in the way that they communicate."

The facilitation challenge in presentation meetings is to avoid these pitfalls. Richardson concludes, "Customers are very savvy about being 'sold to' and have little tolerance for it today. Our behaviors have to clearly show our openness and collaboration, without necessarily agreeing with the customer." [5]

As discussed in more detail in chapter 3, focus on the following:

- being passionate about your insight or solution
- influencing and persuading decision makers
- inspiring action

Conflict-Resolution Meetings

Conflict—any form of disagreement, objection, pushback, or resistance by the buyer—can happen at any time in a meeting or at any point in the sales cycle. How these exchanges are handled can define a relationship with an existing buyer or end the potential for a new one. In these moments, rather than staying present, we can experience the classic fight, flight, or freeze moment.

In the fight response, the sales professional's reaction might come across as aggressive in response to the buyer's behavior. The buyer experiences the behavior as aggressive because the sales professional may choose to reiterate more forcefully the points he or she has already made in reaction to a negative comment from the buyer. It is seen as aggressive because the sales professional stops listening and paying attention to the buyer and instead pushes harder for the sale.

The flight response is the impulse to get away from the buyer as quickly as possible by ending the meeting and avoiding further discussion of the buyer's concerns or frustrations. It's our instinctive urge to get away from the source of our discomfort—the pushy or angry buyer. Yes, I did hang up the phone on screaming clients early in my career. It didn't help matters. In hindsight, the bigger question is why I let the interaction get that far out of hand. Rookie behavior.

The freeze response, on the extreme, is to be rendered speechless, to be unable to come up with any response in the moment. There are many factors that play into such a freeze response in the face of a perceived provocation by the buyer, including the degree of provocation, the experience of the sales professional, or his preexisting stress level caused by other pressures in his career or personal life. Whatever the cause, it's the moment in the meeting when, in hindsight, you cannot believe you were unable to think about any reasonable response! It's the long, pregnant pause at the meeting when you anxiously observe your own brain unable to formulate a response. The appropriate response comes to you readily on your journey home or later in the day, after a conference call ended, when you have had time to calm your triggered nervous system.

None of the fight, flight, or freeze approaches helps us navigate through whatever has caused our buyer to resist—certainly not if you want a long-term relationship. There is a time to be passionate and emotionally expressive. It's not at the moment when the buyer is unwilling to move forward and you don't know why. Your orientation needs to shift back to one of curiosity—about what you missed, what has changed, or what else lies behind their reluctance to move forward. Then, armed with that new information, you can formulate and present your response.

These challenging conversations are opportunities to demonstrate your buyer focus and problem-solving skills, and, if the issue is resolved satisfactorily, to strengthen and deepen the buyer-seller relationship. Yet we often fall on a sword in these moments.

Why does this happen? It can be difficult, for example, not to defend your hard work or your customer-service team who are working overtime to satisfy a demanding buyer, when that buyer expresses dissatisfaction or frustration with the experience.

Many years ago, when I worked in private wealth management, I was sitting at my desk, working. It was close to seven in the evening when my phone rang. I started with my usual greeting, but it was interrupted by a screaming, expletive-ridden male voice on the other end.

"You ******* have done it again. I don't know why I work with you. My net worth is down again this quarter. I'm working with a bunch of idiots!" he yelled.

This went on for what felt like several minutes. As I struggled to keep my composure, I felt, at one point, the color draining from my face. It had never happened to me before, so it took me a while to realize what sensation I was experiencing. It is caused by a sudden drop in blood pressure, which can lead to, in the extreme, fainting. It blew my mind that I was having such a reaction. It took all the courage I could muster to keep listening.

Somehow I managed to acknowledge his frustration. I don't remember now what I said to calm him down; nor did I remember an hour after the event. What I do remember is asking him to explain, when he was sufficiently calm, what was going on for him, why he was so angry, and how I could help him.

In actuality, his asset value was down percentagewise less than the overall market, so what we had set out to do was actually working. My instincts told me that this wasn't the point to make while he was so upset. I stayed with him, "talking him down" as they say, and with this approach, a very pertinent piece of information emerged: our client was getting divorced, and this meant his $5 million account was about to become $2.5 million. That was what was really upsetting him. All the market-and fund-related data in the world wouldn't have appeased his hurt and anger. I ended the call by telling him how sorry I was for him losing his marriage and for the financial loss he was experiencing. After the call, I bummed a cigarette

The buyer team knew that they needed to radically reorganize the distribution channels for their range of products. They were uncertain about the where, when and how to change. With the help of the sales professional and her team from a logistics consulting organization, a problem-solving meeting was arranged to "identify innovative distribution channels for _____ range of enterprise solutions." So began a three-hour meeting involving three internal people from the buyer's team and three individuals with a diversity of skills and roles from the seller's organization. The first fifteen minutes of the session included breathing and other theater exercises to loosen participants up both physically and mentally. An oxygenated brain is a more productive organ. Scattered around the room were hats, Groucho Marx glasses, fake mustaches, modeling clay, and other props. It still amazes me that the simple act of putting on a fedora and a pair of goofy glasses can cause a seismic shift in one's perspective on a problem. The flow of ideas, seemingly exhausted, can once again spring to life by assuming the role of a hat-wearing, shortsighted character. The brain is a wondrous thing.

By the meeting's midpoint, having completed a number of activities and exercises, the whiteboards were awash with ideas. Arriving at a workable solution from such a mass of diverse ideas seemed a little overwhelming. The agreement at the beginning of the session was that Francesca, the problem owner and person responsible for implementation, would make the final decision with our input. Using a preplanned points system, we all awarded a score to the ideas we, individually, liked the most. The ideas awarded the most points were the ones we explored more deeply. From this, a solution began to emerge. The team then began to focus their activities on next steps in the planning and implementation of their preferred ideas.

What follows are the typical steps in a problem-solving meeting:

- **Have a Problem Statement.** In a typical problem-solving meeting process, the first task is to create a clear statement of the issue or problem; this is the headline that clearly and concisely identifies the focus of the meeting.
- **Review Background Materials.** The next step in the meeting is to review background materials; this includes any details or data that will help guide the attendees' thinking and may include what's been tried in the past, what has worked and not worked, and so on. Some of this detail may be supplied in advance of the meeting.
- **Idea Generation and Evaluation.** Once the group has a sufficient grasp of the background, they move to the generation and evaluation of ideas. These are the steps where attendees are encouraged to think creatively and offer ideas on how to address the problem.
- **Healthy Debate and Critique.** The traditional creative problem-solving model refers to this step as brainstorming, where ideas are offered, often in rapid-fire format, without judgment or evaluation. The belief is that the emphasis on quantity over quality will ultimately surface the ideal solution. However, research out of the University of California has shown that an environment of healthy debate and critiquing ideas actually creates the most robust and implementable ideas.[8]
- **Create Implementation Plan.** Once the group has identified the best alternative, their work then becomes creating the implementation plan. This includes a

summary of action items, who is responsible for each item, and deadlines for completion, including interim check-in deadlines.

The right presence in the role of facilitator can make this type of meeting fun, creative, and productive. In a problem-solving meeting, focus on the following:

- creating a psychologically safe and collaborative environment
- encouraging creativity
- being flexible in the ways you respond to the unplanned-for or unexpected

Key Takeaways from Meeting Management

Your presence can transform your meeting outcomes. Becoming an effective meeting facilitator is a satisfying and rewarding skill set to have. It takes time and practice to acquire the knowledge and experience that helps you align the right presence and process skills with the meeting type. Adding this skill set to your selling-skills repertoire is another way to convey your unique value to your buyers. Being thoughtful about your presence based on the meeting type will help you do the following:

- remain curious and avoid presenting solutions during a discovery meeting
- be inspiring and persuasive when presenting an insight or solution during a presentation
- stay calm and avoid the stance of "I'm right, you're wrong," during a conflict-resolution meeting
- stay flexible and collaborative during a problem-solving meeting

CHAPTER 5

In this chapter I will:
◆ **Define personal branding**

◆ **Present a case for why you should deliberately create a personal brand**

◆ **Offer a two-part process for building your brand**

PERSONAL BRANDING

He was in his fifties when I met him—tall, charming when he wanted to be, and certain. Certain about his role as one of the most successful salespeople in the investment firm he had worked at for thirty years, self-assured in his role as the unofficial king of the horsey social set in his hometown just north of Boston.

The first time we met, I was walking into a conference room to interview for a sales position at his thoroughbred-racehorse-investment company in downtown Boston. What struck me most was what he wore. The whole package—suit, tie, monogrammed shirt, and patent-leather shoes—screamed success, wealth, and power, and he fully embraced it.

On several occasions, I witnessed him commanding the attention of a group of mega-wealthy prospects and clients. He charmed them all at once, having them listen attentively to his views on something or other, while he would from time to time teasingly verbally jab one of them or acknowledge something special or unique about another's accomplishments. Sporadically, the whole group would roar with laughter. Bob Singleton knew what his personal brand was, and he lived it every single day of his work life. I'm not advocating for monogrammed shirts; it's not my thing. It did, however, fit the world in which he moved so readily.

WHAT IS PERSONAL BRANDING?

Identifying your personal brand is a necessary and valuable exercise. It's about how you want to be known and understood by your buyers and within your organization and industry. To build a personal brand, you must know your authentic self—your goals, passions, and values. So, it begins with self-awareness. This chapter will help you cultivate your personal brand.

As a sales professional, identifying and becoming explicit and deliberate about how you want to be perceived will help guide your actions. It will help you decide how you want to dress, behave, and interact with others, and it will inform your decision making about the type of buyer you wish to prospect and engage. Being very clear about your personal brand can also accelerate your ascension to a sales career that best suits who you are.

It is important to understand that the brand you craft and the impression you seek to make—how you want people to perceive you and feel about you—must represent *you*. For most, it is easier said than done. Bill George, in his book *Finding Your True North*, says of knowing our authentic self, "knowing ourselves at the deepest level is not easy, as we are complex human beings with many aspects to our character.

We are constantly evolving, as we test ourselves in the world, are influenced by it, and adapt to our environment—all in an attempt to find our unique place."[1]

Much of the work of cultivating your personal brand is an internal journey. It will be helpful to think of this journey in four parts:

i.   Initially work to understand yourself by deepening your understanding of the things that have shaped you, your motivations, and your aspirations.

ii. Then make explicit your values and beliefs.

iii. Next, craft a personal brand statement and create a clear image in your mind of how you want people to respond to you.

iv. Then you can be conscious and explicit about what you wish to become and how you want to show up in the world professionally. You can then use formative personal and professional stories to express who you are and what you value.

First, let's look at a way to help you begin to understand who you are and what your values and beliefs are. Then I'll show you how to develop a personal brand statement. What follows is a structure to enable you to begin to excavate the memories, experiences, and other influences that have created your character. Then you can consciously and explicitly begin to develop your brand.

The benefits of doing this work include being able to

•   identify what's important to you as a sales professional;

- articulate what you stand for, helping clients trust and follow you; and
- motivate buyers with more than just facts and data—be inspiring.

Self-Awareness

The more self-aware you become—knowing what your story is, your strengths and your challenges—the better you can understand and manage a number of aspects of your personal brand, including the following.

The type of selling role that best suits you. This can include, for example, how you feel about and respond to the challenge of acquiring new buyers versus the dynamics of nurturing and deepening an existing relationship, or shorter sales cycles versus longer sales cycles that may take several years of effort before you complete a deal.

Develop relational skills. The better you know and understand yourself, the more comfortable you can become in your own skin. Most sales professionals are in this career because they have relational skills in abundance.

A young up-and-coming financial adviser I was coaching told me that when he sat in meetings with ultra-wealthy people, many of them billionaires, he noticed that his face became flushed, which caused him to become even more flustered and therefore feel incapable of making a worthwhile contribution to the meeting. He told me the self-critical voice in his head was saying, *Why would these hugely successful people have any interest in what I have to say?* As we continued to talk and explore what was happening for him in these moments, it emerged that he had grown up in a humble setting in rural America, so meeting with mega-rich Americans triggered feelings of shame for him because of the environment of poverty in which he was raised. This was the beginning place for helping him learn to relax more by seeing his clients as fellow human beings first and connecting with them at that level.

It is from a foundation of knowing how you respond in different situations that you can identify the behaviors that are helpful to you and those that get in the way of your success. Knowing what these are and being conscious about how and why you are responding this way, in other words, beginning to understand and correctly label the underlying feelings, is the beginning of control over the behaviors.

In the example above, it was difficult for the investment adviser to admit to me—and four of his peers who were also present—that he was having such difficulty with wealthy clients. He was working in a pretty unforgiving corporate culture. His willingness to be honest and vulnerable was the beginning place for addressing the necessary behavior change.

An Authentic You. There's an old Woody Allen movie called *Zelig* where the main character, because of his low self-esteem and a desire to fit in and be liked, takes on the characteristics of whatever strong character he's around. Such a chameleon-like existence being parodied by Allen in the movie struck a chord with me as a sales professional. I recognized myself in Zelig. Sometimes I tried too hard to flex to the buyer. The cost of this was not being "seen" and maybe even being perceived as pandering or inauthentic. Bob Singleton knew exactly who he was and the buyers to whom he wanted to appeal. It certainly was not about being all things to everyone for him!

A Two-Part Process for Building Your Brand

The following exercises will help you explore who you are, what you value, and how you want to be known. Ultimately, it will help you convey your brand in interactions with buyers and understand how you can leverage your values to deepen your relationships with them. It will also help you craft and use formative personal and professional stories to express who you are and what you value. Take your time with the following exercises. Cultivating and articulating your brand is not a simple task. I suggest you work on this in the following way.

Part 1. Self-Awareness and Insight
Step One. Your Strengths and Growing Edges

i. Strengths

Begin with an honest inventory of your strengths and skills. A strength could be your natural ability to connect with others and nurture a long-term relationship, or it could be an ability to present complex information in a way that is understandable to a less technically minded audience. The goal is to identify what you are instinctively or most naturally good at and the skills you have to help you take advantage of that strength. Skills may include facilitation or negotiation skills, for example.

An example of how to think about your strengths is exemplified in the following brief story. I was at a sales-training event at a large financial-services organization. I noticed a sales professional in the group, Jeff, who was at least twenty years older than the average age of his peers. During lunch, I sat down with him, and during our conversation, I asked him why he had stayed in this career for so long. He began by telling me that he had recently returned from vacation with one of his clients. He explained that his biggest clients are like family to him because of the depth and quality of the relationships. He said he was as energized to come to work now as he was twenty-five years ago. He was fascinated and sometimes frustrated by the changes in the industry, and he continued to learn new things.

Jeff spent a few minutes bemoaning the requirements and paperwork he had to complete on a regular basis to adhere to stringent compliance requirements. "It's a real frustration for me, and when this stuff gets in the way of closing deals, it pushes me over the edge," he added. Jeff was relaxed and disarmingly funny at times.

From this example, it is possible to distill Jeff's strengths and skills:

- builds meaningful relationships
- expresses himself authentically
- evolves skills as industry evolves
- connects using humor and a sense of fun

Your Strengths and Skills
Briefly describe your strengths and skills as a sales professional:

_____

_____

_____

_____

_____

ii. Growing Edges
Now identify your growing edges. These are the things that get in the way of being the best you want to be or know you can be. It can be something you have come to understand about

yourself through self-reflection or feedback from a buyer, boss, peer, or loved one.

Examples of a growing edge could be managing work-life integration more effectively or learning to say no. These are things you know, which if successfully addressed, will improve your performance.

For Jeff, these could be

- learning to be more patient and
- recovering more quickly when deals don't close.

Your Growing Edges
Briefly describe your growing edges as a sales professional:

_____

_____

_____

_____

_____

_____

Step Two. Life-Shaping Stories—Personal and Professional

There are events that have informed who you have become as you have grown and developed. I am inviting you to go deep here. The things that shape us are the major life events, both wonderful and tragic. They can be events like the loss of a loved one, a sporting victory, or overcoming a challenge in your personal life such as a serious illness. Events and challenges have also helped shape your career. My own example is my father's untimely death, launching my career in business at a young age. That event left a lasting mark that has shaped my beliefs, honed my ambitions, and greatly influenced my values.

I was working with a sales professional in the technology industry. She told me the story of learning an important lesson early in her career about negotiating. She was in the middle of a negotiation for the largest deal on her organization's books at the time. She had, over the previous nine months, navigated through the sales cycle, beginning with an initial RFP. Everything, including a draft implementation plan, was in place. The buyer asked for a price reduction in a contract line item. The sales professional negotiated internally and got support to allow the price reduction. The buyer then asked for another and another eventually asking for and receiving a half dozen line-item price reductions across the range of agreed-upon services. The sales professional had fought hard internally, burning a few bridges along the way, to get support for the price reductions.

When the deal was completed and the services implemented, she asked for a debrief meeting with the buyer. As they began the meeting, the buyer offhandedly admitted that he and his team had been ready to sign off on the deal at the originally agreed prices but had been happy and somewhat amused by her willingness to respond to his line-item price-reduction requests so late in the deal.

Her lesson was learning to find a balance between being responsive to the buyer and doing the right thing for her employer by more effectively selling the value of their services.

Capture the details of two life-shaping stories from your past, one personal and one professional.

Personal:

_____

_____

_____

Professional:

_____

_____

_____

Step Three. Your Role Models

Here you should think about two role models whose characteristics, traits, or styles you wish to emulate. These are people who have helped you develop and grow. When you are in a jam, you wonder, what would this person do? It could be a sports coach, a relative who had an influential role in your upbringing, or a former boss or mentor. Identify what it is about them that you emulate or would like to emulate. This could include their style, relational skills—the way they treat people, their orientation to life and work, and so on. In other words, what have they got that you like and have embraced or would like to embrace?

For roughly the first fifteen years of my career, I tended to show up differently with buyers, depending on where they resided in the corporate hierarchy. When I was meeting with people nearer the front line of the organization, I tended to show up as more of my true self—more relaxed and engaging. At the upper end of the corporate ladder, when meeting with C-suite people, I tended to be deferential, coy, and overly careful. It could be perceived as being professional, but a consequence of this "professionalism" was that it didn't allow me to connect at a more personal level.

The experiences of working with my wife, Amy, an executive coach, and observing her ability to be her authentic self regardless of the wealth, power, or authority of the other person with whom she's working, have helped me hone the skill of more consistently being myself, whatever the setting.

Amy says of herself that she gives others an A upon meeting them. She assumes the best in others will show more readily if she conveys a warmth and genuine interest in who they are and what they have to offer the world.

Characteristics, Traits, and Behaviors of Those You Wish to Emulate

Make a list of the things you wish to emulate:

_____

_____

_____

_____

Step Four. Greatest Accomplishments—Personal and Professional

Bucket List—Personal and Professional

This requires you to identify two accomplishments for which you feel particularly proud—ideally one accomplishment from your personal life and one from your professional life. It could be meeting and falling in love with your partner, a sporting victory, or landing your first job or closing the biggest deal of your career. Next, identify your bucket list, personal and professional. This is your wish list for goals you would like to achieve, or things you would like to do before you die.

Greatest Accomplishments
Professional:

_____

_____

_____

Personal:

_____

_____

_____

Bucket List

Professional:

Personal:

Step Five. Determine Your Emotional Appeal

An important step in building your self-awareness is to determine your emotional appeal. To continue your work in cultivating your personal brand, take some time to identify how others perceive you and how you feel they benefit by working with you.

Think of a particular selling situation, and use the following questions to guide your thinking.

How do I believe I make people feel?

How do people benefit by working with me?

_____

_____

_____

What adjectives might others use to describe me?

_____

_____

_____

Part 2. Cultivating Your Brand

Step One. Working with a Partner to Clarify Your Personal Brand

When you have completed the work outlined in part 1, it will be helpful to take some time to interpret and make meaning of it, to help distill your values and begin to determine the components what will make up your brand. From the work above, you now have a collection of data. I am suggesting that you come up with a personal brand statement that translates all the above data into a concise, meaningful message that captures the essence of you and the specifics of what you stand for.

For this stage of cultivating your brand, it will be most helpful if you work with someone who knows you and whose opinion you trust. We need help from other people to understand our own personal brand deeply. It will be helpful if you could share steps one through five from part one with your partner, who will be listening with the intention of helping you clarify your values, your value, and your goals. Your partner can respond to your stories and help you make meaning of them. With this partner, make time, ideally a couple of hours, to do the following in detail.

Share part one, steps one through five.

1. **Strengths and Growing Edges**
2. **Life-Shaping Stories:** One personal and one professional
3. **Role Models:** Characteristics and traits
4. **Greatest Accomplishments and Bucket List:** one personal and one professional of each
5. **Seek feedback about your emotional appeal**

When you have finished these steps, it is time to ask your partner to respond to what he or she has heard. Ask your partner the following questions:

- What core values and strengths do you hear?
- Which of the stories you heard do you imagine would help my clients know they want to work with me?

With the help of your partner to clarify what is most important to you, the next step is to use this information to craft your personal brand statement.

Step Two. Create a Personal Brand Statement

Your job now is to bring your brand alive through the stories you tell and the values they illustrate. According to *Psychology Today*, telling stories is the best way to teach and persuade. Telling stories is a significant part of your role as a sales professional. With this in mind, craft a personal story you can use with buyers. It should be no more than three minutes long. In that time, convey something important about who you are, your values, and what motivates you as a sales professional. When used in the right context, these stories help build connection.

Outlined below is a suggestion for how to distill your personal brand statement through storytelling.

>   **a. Story.** Example: "Let me give me you an example from my personal life. The year is 1984, I am about to go onstage for my first role in the theater troupe in my new college, when I see my uncle standing in the back of the audience. I know immediately that something is very wrong..."

>   **b. Values.** Example: "Two values that guide my role as a sales professional are you can't take anything or anyone for granted..."

>   **c. Conclusion.** "What this mean for our work together is I am direct, honest, and I hate wasting time..."

I heard the following personal brand statement from a sales leader.

I grew up in Texas. We moved there when I was ten, because my parents couldn't find work in Kansas. My father got a job as a laborer, and my mother worked evenings. It was difficult for them, but what I remember most from that time was their dedication to each other and the family. I also remember the fun and laughter that carried us through those times. I was the first in my family to go to college. When I was twenty-two, I went to New York for a job interview. I stayed for a few days and called my parents collect (this was a time before cell phones) each evening to report the events of the day. On the third day, I got a job offer from a large financial institution. It would be my first full-time job. At the end of the day, I excitedly called my family to tell them the news. My father listened patiently as I described my job. He paused when I had finished, not really understanding the work I had described. He eventually said, "Does this mean you won't be calling collect anymore?" We both laughed. So what you will get if you work with me is an incredibly strong work ethic, a sense of humor, and my appreciation for the value of your hard-earned money.

It can be helpful to develop several stories and have them in your back pocket, ready to use depending on the situation.

Your Appearance

If my wife were looking over my shoulder as I wrote the above heading, she would say something like "You are not qualified to tell anyone how to improve his or her appearance!" And she'd be correct, because outward appearance is not something that I inherently value—but I have learned. I had to. So, what follows are some thoughts, ideas, and best practices related to aligning your appearance with your brand.

The first indicators of my presence in a face-to-face interaction with my buyers are my physical appearance, posture, and dress. My look is an integral part of my brand, so I put some thought into what I wear. Thinking about my appearance is not my favorite way to spend time. Over the years, I have come to appreciate spending time on my appearance because I know that others are forming an opinion about me based on it. My goal with my appearance is to stand out in a positive way.

Appearance is an important component of your overall presence. It is the visual cue that can help you more fully embrace your role and put your best foot forward. For me, putting on a well-tailored suit and tie causes me to improve my posture and project a sense of poise and self-assurance.

Here are some ideas and tips on how to have a dress code that's tied to your personal brand:

- Choose clothing that matches and enhances your authentic self. Create a look, own it, and wear it. If you would like to communicate vibrancy and innovation, your look should reflect this!
- Choose a look that resonates with your industry. For example, if you are in a young, hip industry, create a look that is distinctive and appeals to the audience with whom you need to connect and influence.
- Your hairstyle, grooming, and use of makeup should also fit the brand image you are conveying.
- Use accessories that complement your signature brand. It could be a watch or a piece of jewelry.

Sometimes it's trial and error, as the following story conveys. My family and I visit my wife's mother in Florida every winter. Though the warm weather is always a welcome break from the New England winter, the slow pace of life in my aging mother-in-law's community can become mind numbing. So my wife and I created an annual ritual of a night out in Delray Beach. The ritual includes mojitos and late-night shopping. This is a bad combination if you pride yourself on being an otherwise-thrifty shopper. It was on one of these cocktail-fueled shopping sprees that I discovered the Bugatchi brand, particularly their shirts. If you are familiar with this brand, then you can probably speed-read this section! Their shirts are described as elegant with eye-catching patterns and colors.

Some weeks after the purchase, I was packing my bag for a business trip to a financial organization I had been working with for several years. In a moment of "what the heck," I grabbed the Bugatchi and headed out. On day two of my visit,

I donned the eye-catching patterned shirt and walked to the client's New York office. As I entered the meeting room to say good morning to the usual cast of characters for this meeting, one of them, well known for his "shoot first, ask questions later" style, spotted me from the far side of the room. Like an eagle locked in on his prey, the client, Jack, moved in for the kill without hesitation. I managed to say "good" before Jack, staring with intent at my shirt, said, "Don't ever wear a shirt like that here again. We wear solid blue or white. That's it." The Bugatchi shirt, still among my favorites, makes appearances when I work with media, tech, or advertising firms. It's Brooks Brothers and blue and white crisp shirts for the financial institutions. I have become quite comfortable, and able to be myself in either attire.

Building a personal brand takes ongoing time and effort. The payback, according to Fastcompany, is that there "is a clear correlation between success and branding." Having a business degree, for example, is no longer a distinguishing feature; it's your ticket to the game. Being thoughtful and deliberate about who you are and how you want to be in your sales career will give you the frame of reference for how you handle yourself and treat others. It is "as much about consistently delivering on your promise as it is about differentiation."[2] Being clear about your personal brand is an easy way to differentiate yourself from the pack.

CHAPTER 6

In this chapter I will:

◆ Demonstrate why having a social media presence is a necessity in sales

◆ Discuss how to build and maintain your social media presence

◆ Present, in a step-by-step fashion, how to build and maintain your social media presence on LinkedIn, Twitter, Facebook and Instagram

YOUR SOCIAL MEDIA PRESENCE

In the late 1990s, during the first Internet boom, there were dire predictions about the future of the sales profession. In a matter of years, the profession would be obsolete, replaced by interactive, friendly avatars and easy-to-navigate websites that would make the selection of the correct solution uncomplicated. The power would be firmly in the hands of the buyer. Curiously, the number of people employed in sales and sales-related roles as a percentage of the workforce actually increased during this period, according to the US Bureau of Labor Statistics. [1] Anecdotally, buyers at the end of the twentieth century actually needed more help navigating a rapidly changing and more complex buyer/seller world. This is a complexity born of the shift from traditional buying methodologies in a relatively stable environment, to one where the Internet and technological innovation actually added to the difficulty of making the right choice. Buyers needed help and reassurance from informed sales professionals.

Fast forward to 2015, when Forrester Research predicted that one million B2B salespeople would become obsolete by 2020.[2] So, what are buyers doing now that makes it possible for them to rely less on sales professionals for help and guidance? More importantly, what do sales professionals need to do to stay ahead of the competition and stay relevant to their buyers?

THE PARADIGM SHIFT IN BUYER BEHAVIOR

CEB research concludes that buyers "are readily turning to their personal networks and publicly available information—increasingly via digital and social media channels—to self-diagnose their problems and form opinions about solutions."[3] This is what they are doing to self-manage through the first 60 percent of the traditional sales cycle or purchasing process. In fact, 72 percent of buyers use social media before making a purchase, according to DemandGen a business-intelligence firm.[4] According to LinkedIn, 81 percent are more likely to engage a sales professional with a strong, professional brand.[5]

By the time they engage a sales professional, buyers have likely completed the following due diligence:

- identified possible solution providers through a network or Google search
- reviewed offerings by reading website content, including blogs, white papers, testimonials, and case studies
- understood how a solution would work generically by watching a video demonstration

- visited forums and other social-media sites to gather data from end users on the quality of the providers' solutions, service levels, reputation, etc.
- filtered potential providers down to the top three or four

Source: SalesHub[6]

Then the buyers engage the sales professional to further problem solve, inform, and educate themselves before making a final decision. The shift in power from seller to buyer is significant.

Consider the last time you bought a car. You likely researched the price of the make and model, checked the ratings of the dealership, and possibly looked up the social media ratings for the car-sales professionals on a site like dealerrater.com. You then had the option to ask for a specific sales professional when you walked onto the dealership's lot, based on the quality of the reviews you read. That is what's happening across industries, whether it's directly from individual seller to individual buyer, business to consumer, or business to business.

What follows are things to consider when building an online presence, a presence that's focused on communicating to your potential buyers "I'm an expert and am here and willing to help you when you're ready." It's about building credibility, trust, and a connection with buyers digitally, making you an obvious choice when your buyer is ready to talk.

BUILDING AND MAINTAINING A SOCIAL MEDIA PRESENCE

Your social media presence is an extension of your personal brand. It is another medium in which you can differentiate yourself by authentically communicating your unique value proposition. It is necessary to have consistency and congruency between your live and your virtual business and personal presence. It's necessary because a well-crafted empathic and engaging social media presence that's exposed as inauthentic when a live conversation or meeting takes place will not only potentially undermine your credibility with that buyer, but it can also harm your brand within your broader network, if the buyer chooses to post a negative review about his or her experience with you and your organization.

When you set out to establish and maintain a social media presence, it is important to consider what you post, repost, like, and Retweet. You want your social media presence to convey what is unique and valuable about you as a sales professional, help you establish your credibility, and build trust so you can influence your buyer to react in a favorable way to you and your organization. The problem is it takes time and thought. It takes time to consistently expend effort thoughtfully creating or locating appropriate posts, responding to questions and posts from your target buyers without the immediate gratification of having a lead to put in your pipeline. Like all prospecting, it can feel like a Sisyphean task, but done with a long-term view, the effort will be rewarded.

Building your social media presence should focus on LinkedIn, Twitter, Facebook, and Instagram. What follows are key guidelines and suggestions on how best to leverage these platforms.

LINKEDIN

I was recently with a sales professional as she sat at her desk working. I noticed she was on LinkedIn and asked how she used it. Her answer was immediate. "I can't imagine being in sales and not using LinkedIn. I use it for so many things now. From identifying and connecting with decision makers and influencers at my target accounts to using my network to frequently end up with a warm referral. It really has made how I sell easier."

No one explains how a sales professional can leverage LinkedIn better than LinkedIn. Here are their top ten tips for leveraging their network, validated by LinkedIn members.

Sales tip #1: Create an effective executive profile

Don't let your LinkedIn profile read like a résumé. Customize your LinkedIn experience by:

- **Uploading a professional photo:** You are eleven times more likely to have your LinkedIn profile viewed if you have a picture.
- **Writing a compelling headline:** Add your job title, current company, and a tagline about how you help customers.
- **Adding a summary:** Your summary, in essence, is "the story of you." Share the vision you have for your role or company.
- **Adding rich media like videos and presentations:** You'll maximize your exposure on LinkedIn and better showcase your story.

Sales tip #2: Efficiently connect with the people who matter

LinkedIn isn't intended to replace face-to-face interactions; instead, it optimizes your ability to know more about people you've met or are about to meet. Also, inviting people to connect is a great way to follow up on an in-person meeting.

Sales tip #3: Leverage your mutual connections

People are five times more likely to engage with you if the outreach is through a mutual connection. See who within your network is connected to your second- or third-degree connections, and request an introduction.

Sales tip #4: Find your top-tier customers

Sales is about people, but nurturing relationships takes time. LinkedIn allows you to find your customers by searching by name, company, or position, so you can easily connect and establish better relationships.

Sales tip #5: Follow your customers' activity in real time

If you are connected with your customers, their public activity will appear in your newsfeed. Keep tabs on your contacts' interests and updates so you can remain top of mind and provide them necessary information.

Sales tip #6: Listen to conversations and debate

Joining and following group discussions in your industry is an excellent way to gain customer insights about needs, interests, and more.

Sales tip #7: Use LinkedIn Pulse to stay on top of industry trends

LinkedIn Pulse curates content in real time, based on your interests and the companies and influencers you follow. Share and comment on these articles to demonstrate your insights.

Sales tip #8: Reach people directly and more credibly with InMail

Effective sales prospecting requires communicating in a way that gets noticed. Identify something personal about the person that you can reference in the message. Then send a follow up InMail one to two weeks after the original; it increases the response rate by 500 percent.

Sales tip #9: Engage with your customers

Today there are more than 1.5 million unique publishers actively sharing content on LinkedIn. You can become a voice in your industry by sharing relevant blog posts, insights, and industry news.

Sales tip #10: Publish content

Leverage LinkedIn's publishing platform to share long-form posts with your network and beyond. When you publish a post on LinkedIn, your content becomes part of your profile and is shared with everyone, even those outside of your network.

Source: LinkedIn[7]

Your Presence on LinkedIn Forums and Message Boards

Finding prospects in an active buying mode is an exciting moment for a sales professional. For me, it is similar to the feeling I get when I spot a trout breaking the surface of a river on a warm spring evening while I am walking the bank with my fly rod in hand. The probability of some action just increased significantly!

So, when a sales professional spots a potential buyer "break the surface" by posting a query to a group chat that implies an interest in what the sales professional is selling, the temptation to jump in with "Here's what we offer that can help you" is understandable. However, just like me when I am fly fishing, the sales professional needs to figure out the best approach to attract the 'feeding' buyer. He needs to avoid coming on too strong too quickly with an ill-timed pitch.

We need to build credibility and trust by being thought partners who are collaborative problem solvers and sources of industry-relevant knowledge, rather than pushy salespeople looking for a quick deal. We need to build solid relational foundations. Here is how we can do it.

- *Join groups.* Identify and become a part of active industry-related groups where your targeted buyers will go to seek and share information.
- *Get involved in conversations.* Identify any rules the group has established, and get involved in conversations, ask and answer questions, and monitor the responses you get. Your intention is to get noticed for the right reasons. Craft intelligent responses that thoughtfully answer the question being asked. You want to showcase your expertise.
- *Avoid being "salesy."* Avoid shameless self-promotion or pitching your products or solutions. Groups are formed with the intention of being a source for collaborative and supportive discussions. Your buyers join these groups to seek help through advice and information from industry peers and other subject-matter experts. Posting a sales pitch will more than likely turn them off. The opportunity to engage in a consultative sales conversation will happen after you have established a connection based on your desire to help, rather than your drive to sell. If you get to this level of relationship with a buyer, you can take the conversation offline.

Let's imagine "Arielle" posts on a group chat: "I am a sales-competency manager at a large technology company, and I am having difficulty providing impactful sales training. Should I be tracking attendance, making it mandatory, or change the design of the program?"

Avoid posts like: "Hi, Arielle. I read your post. I'd like to invite you to try out our sales-training app, 'SalesBlast.' you can find it in the app store of Apple and the Google Play store. It's a gamified sales training app ..."

Craft posts like: "Hi Arielle, I wonder if you know the reasons why participants try to avoid the training in the first place? I'm wondering if tracking attendance might be a Band-Aid. Have you considered running a small focus group with a cross-section of sales professionals, to ask them what they need to have in a learning experience that will help them acquire the right skills so they can be more effective? What do you think of that? If that is interesting to you I'd be happy to share some experiences I have had when doing this for my own business."

TWITTER

Though Twitter is not a professional network like LinkedIn, it plays a significant role in the activity and success of the contemporary sales professional. According to salesforce.com, B2B companies that use Twitter get twice as many sales leads compared to those that don't.[8]

Like LinkedIn, the goal of being active on Twitter is to participate in the most relevant conversations as they happen, identify opportunities before your competitors do, connect and build relationships with buyers, and build your personal brand.

Here are some of the rules for using Twitter to grow your sales:

- *Identify and follow prospective and existing buyers.*
  Go through the mundane process of searching Twitter
  to find the names and organizations of those with whom
  you already do business and those you are targeting.
  Remember, your best prospect is an existing client, so
  keep your finger on their pulse while you look for new
  opportunities.
- *Monitor for opportunities.* Monitor your following list
  for opportunities to respond with useful information.
  This will help deepen your connections, build your
  profile, and help you respond to live sales opportunities.
  Specific opportunities may arise from an individual's
  feed; you may also gather important information by
  following the organization's feed. Take a holistic approach
  to whom you follow at your targeted organizations.
  This will increase your opportunities to gather
  valuable background information. Then, when you do
  get the opportunity to meet with buyers, referencing
  this public information will make your insights and
  presentations more relevant and more persuasive.
- *Build and maintain your own following.* Establish your
  credibility by building a significant following of your
  own. Start by creating a professional and focused bio
  that represents your own, and your employer's brand.
  Salesforce recommends that you "Tweet often; a few
  times a day during the working day is a minimum.
  The more you tweet, the more followers you will get.
  Live tweets about events you're attending using the
  official hashtag can help draw a following. Comment
  on topical subjects that are relevant to your product/
  brand, making a connection between news of the day
  and your company."

Similar to being active on LinkedIn groups, your orientation on Twitter is to become a helpful, supportive subject-matter expert in the eyes of your buyers. For example, demonstrating your desire to be helpful by retweeting a question to your followers will help build trust and your credibility.

FACEBOOK

Using Facebook as part of your social-media presence-building strategy needs a softer approach than LinkedIn, and here's why: in a Hubspot survey of buyers and consumers, 78 percent said receiving a friend request from a salesperson would weird them out. An even higher percentage, 81 percent, said getting a Facebook message from a salesperson fell into the "creepy" category.[9]

There are ways to leverage Facebook successfully. Alice Myerhoff, author of *Social Media for Sales People*, an outstanding resource for social-media selling, makes the following recommendations:

1. *Like your buyers' Facebook business pages.* This is a great way to stay on top of what those businesses are talking about in public, which can help you understand what they are trying to accomplish. If they post something interesting, you can share it and possibly build up your profile with them.

2. *Organize your Facebook friends into custom lists.* Create a list for current customers and clients that you are already connected to in Facebook. Create a second list of potential customers and clients. Creating these lists allows you to isolate the posts from the people you put on these lists and quickly add your voice to the conversations they are having on FB by commenting on posts or sharing their posts.

3. *Try out a search using Facebook graph.* Using this feature you can find out which of your friends work at a certain company, or if they have friends that work for that company.

4. *Post something related to your work.* As long as you keep 80 percent of your posts personal in nature, you can do some posting about what's happening at your work. Of course, keep things positive.

5. *Like some media pages related to your work.* Search for the business pages of some of the media companies in your area of business, as well as some general media companies. This sets you up to be able to share useful content with your Facebook network.[10]

Facebook may be viewed as a treasure trove of prospects, but tread carefully, as your intention is to build a presence that is credible and trustworthy.

As traditional sales and marketing efforts become less and less effective, the sales professionals who embrace social selling as a component of their selling efforts will increase their success. For example, payroll-service company ADP increased its leads worked by sales by 21 percent as a result of its social-selling efforts.[11]

Creating and sustaining an online presence needs to be planned and executed with a collaboration of sales and marketing. Ultimately, every sales professional should have an authentic social media presence, connecting with the right prospects and sharing high-quality content.

As I write this, Instagram is emerging as a valuable medium for sourcing business opportunities. Perhaps by the time you are reading this, other social-media platforms will have emerged in a similar vein. Here are some tips for leveraging Instagram in your selling efforts:

1. Build visibility in the news feed. This can be achieved by nurturing followers who care enough about your business to share your posts, leave comments and likes, and tag their friends.

2. Maintain a personal rather than a business account. Interestingly, anecdotal data show that personal profiles are indexed higher than business accounts.

3. Create a sales presence. In your Instagram profile, include a brief brand statement related to your business. You should also consider including representative photos and images.

4. Use hashtags. Instagram limits hashtags to thirty per post. Use hashtags that will attract your ideal buyer audience.

5. Use an appropriate amount of posts based on your targeted buyer audience. While you want to attract and engage your buyers, you need to avoid overwhelming them with posts.

6. Help your buyers solve a problem. Like the other social-media platforms, rather than being perceived as a pushy salesperson, you want to build a connection and help them see you as a problem solver or someone who can make their lives easier.

Whatever the social-media platform on which we engage our buyers, we need to be generous with our knowledge. This is one way buyers size us up, and it's a great statement of our self-confidence that we are willing to share our knowledge and expertise because we have so much more to offer.

CHAPTER 7

In this chapter I will:
◆ **Encourage you to go out there and be the best sales professional you can be**

BE THE DIFFERENCE

The life expectancy of an S&P 500 company was sixty-one years in 1958. According to Innosight, it is now eighteen years.[1]

Industries, organizations, and their products have an ever-shortening life expectancy. We live in an era of what change-management guru John Kotter describes as "a white water of change." Buyers are painfully aware of the need to stay ahead of the changes happening in their respective industries. Sales professionals are well positioned to become "the eyes on the industry," offering perspectives, ideas, and insights to their buyers.

CEB's book *The Challenger Sale: Taking Control of the Customer Conversation* has captured the attention and imagination of sales leaders around the world. While promoting a more aggressive approach to selling, it concurrently denigrates the traditional consultative-sales methodology as being no longer relevant.

Their research shows that the profiles of sales professionals who succeed in a complex sale in this environment are what they call Challengers. The primary characteristics of these sales professionals are that they think differently, take control of the sale from the beginning, are willing to debate and provoke their buyer's thinking, and know the buyer's problems better than the buyer does. CEB says that sales professionals who sell in this way are *4.5 times more likely* to be high performers in a complex sales environment.[2]

Words like "debate" and "provoke" and the suggestion that you know the buyer's problems better than the buyer does can lead you down a slippery slope with the potential to derail qualified opportunities by being perceived as being too pushy, arrogant, or insensitive. The differentiator here is presence. *Forbes* magazine reported on a survey that revealed "emotional value overwhelmingly outweighed logic and reason in driving purchase decisions."[3]

Great presence is the key to allowing us to be direct while creating a feeling in our buyers that we are credible, caring, smart, interested, and that we value the individual or people with whom we are dealing.

Presence Transcends Process

Like the sales professionals who engage them, buyers are a diverse and complex collection of humans. Being human means we have different needs and wants, exhibit a variety of personality traits and characteristics, have good days and bad days, and work in a variety of corporate cultures. Our effectiveness as sales professionals is contingent on our ability to adapt our presences to bring our best selling selves to our interactions with these buyers consistently over time.

Edward R. Murrow, who pioneered TV news journalism at CBS and whose legacy was cemented in the movie *Good Night and Good Luck* once said of journalism, "To be persuasive, we must be believable; to be believable, we must be credible; to be credible, we must be truthful." The same can be said of our profession.

Truthfulness begins with an honest self-assessment—what are your presence strengths and weaknesses—so that you can leverage your strengths (characteristics, behaviors, skills) and selectively address your weaknesses. Consider again the list from chapter 1 of what a great presence allows you to do. Use it as a checklist as you develop and hone a set of skills and behaviors that will set you apart in an increasingly competitive and demanding profession.

I was working with a group of sales professionals in the medical-device industry, and we were discussing managing some of the difficult clients of this particular organization. One member of the group told the story of his ongoing e-mail exchange with a particularly belligerent client. "I'm ready to tear my hair out!" he exclaimed at one point.

One of his peers said in response, "Dude, you gotta go see him and talk this out, or at least get on the phone."

"That sounds exhausting" was his immediate reply.

In a task-oriented, goal-driven world where time and energy feel like such scarce resources, making time to bring your best most present self to your busy, metric-driven role can seem daunting and unnecessary. From my own point of view and experience, I say yes, it takes time and energy, *and* it is worth it. It is worth it because of the quality of interactions that can emerge and the increase in the deals these interactions will yield. So, rather than take my word for it, why not challenge yourself to try some of the things I have presented in this book? Maybe invite some honest feedback about your presence from someone whose opinion you trust, attend a selling-presence program, take an improvisational acting class, spend time thinking about and crafting your personal brand, and make the time to be more active on social media, focusing on your business-development activities.

I sincerely hope you are willing to work on your presence so you can close more deals. We have so much power to affect other people positively; let's use it to give our buyers the best insights and solutions we can possibly give. My willingness to work on my presence has not only given me a more meaningful career, but also a tremendous sense of pride in our profession. Wherever you are in your career, I wish you success or continued success.

ENDNOTES

Introduction

1 Schmidt, Karl; Adamson, Brent; Bird, Anna (2015) Making the Consensus Sale. Harvard Business Review, Reprint R1503H
2 Spenner, Patrick; Schmidt, Karl 2015, March, 31. Two Numbers You Should Care About. Retrieved from https://www.cebglobal.com/blogs/b2b-sales-and-marketing-two-numbers-you-should-care-about/
3 Schultz, Mike and Doerr, John E. (2014). Insight Selling: Surprising Research on What Sales Winners Do Differently. Hoboken, New Jersey: John Wiley & Sons
4 Porges, Stephen W. (2011). The Polyvagal Theory. New York, NY: W.W. Norton & Co.

Chapter 1

1 Goleman, Daniel (2005) Emotional Intelligence: Why It Can Matter More Than IQ. New York, NY: Bantam Dell, A Division of Random House
2 Goleman, Daniel (2006) Social Intelligence: The New Science of Human Relationships. New York, NY: Bantam Dell, A Division of Random House
3 Stone and Heen (2015) Thanks For The Feedback: The Science and Art of Receiving Feedback Well. New York, NY: Penguin Group
4 Groppel, Jack (2000) The Corporate Athlete: How to Achieve Maximal Performance in Business and Life. New York, NY: John Wiley & Sons, Inc,

5   Mayo Clinic Staff (2014, July 19).Meditation: A Simple Fast Way To Reduce Stress. Retrieved from http://www.mayoclinic.org/tests-procedures/meditation/in-depth/meditation/art-20045858

6   Porges, Stephen W. (2011). The Polyvagal Theory. New York, NY: W.W. Norton & Co.

Chapter 2

1   Goleman, Daniel (2006) Social Intelligence: The New Science of Human Relationships. New York, NY: Bantam Dell, A Division of Random House

2   Edmonson, Amy (1999) Psychological Safety and Learning Behavior In Work Teams. Administrative Science Quarterly. Vol. 44 (2) pp. 350-383

3   Buber, Martin (1970). I and Thou. New York, NY: Touchstone

4   Gladwell, Malcolm (2005) Blink: The Power of Thinking Without Thinking. New York, NY: Little, Brown & Company

Chapter 3

1   Grodnitzky and Smalfus (2016) Selling With Insights. Philadelphia, PA: Richardson

2   O'Hara, Carolyn (2014) The Right Way To Present Your Business Case. Boston MA: Harvard Business Review

3   Sandler, David (1995) You Can't Teach A Kid To Ride A Bike At A Seminar. New York, NY: Penguin Books

4   Rock and Schwartz (2015) The Neuroscience of Leadership. New York, NY: Palgrave Macmillan

5   Goleman, Daniel (2015, January 21) A Relax Mind is a Productive Mind. Retrieved from http://www.danielgoleman.info/daniel-golema n-a-relaxed-mind-is-a-productive-mind/

6   Stanislavski, Constantin (1989) An Actor Prepares. New York, NY: Routledge

7   Ekman, Paul (2003) Emotions Revealed. Second Edition. New York, NY: Owl Books

8   Porges, Stephen W. (2011). The Polyvagal Theory. New York, NY: W.W. Norton & Co.

9   Spolin, Viola (2017) Some Spolin Games Used in Performance. Retrieved from http://spolin.com/?page_id=10

10   Cuddy, Amy (2012). Your Body Language Shapes Who You Are. Retrieved from https://www.ted.com/talks/amy_cuddy_your_body_language_shapes_who_you_are

11   Pink, Daniel H. (2012). To Sell Is Human. New York, NY: Penguin Group (USA)

Chapter 4

1   Lencioni, Patrick (2004). Death By Meeting. San Francisco, CA: Jossey-Bass

2   Stone, Patton and Heen (2010) Difficult Conversations: How To Discuss What Matters Most. New York,NY: Penguin Group

3   Adapted from Lou Bergholz (2005). Facilitating Productive Meetings. Publisher: Author

4   Neosperience Team (2015) 10 Inspirational Customer Experience Quotes to Improve Engagement. Retrieved from http://blog.neosperience.com/10-inspirational-customer-experience-quotes-to-improve-engagement

5   Schultz, Mike and Doerr, John E. (2014). Insight Selling: Surprising Research on What Sales Winners Do Differently. Hoboken, New Jersey: John Wiley & Sons

6   Stone, Patton and Heen (2010) Difficult Conversations: How To Discuss What Matters Most. New York,NY: Penguin Group

7   Scott, Susan (2004). Fierce Conversations: Achieving Success at Work and in Life One Conversation at a Time. New York, NY: The Berkley Publishing Group

8   Hult News (2012). Brainstorming or Debate? How About Both? Retrieved from http://www.hult.edu/news/brainstorming-or-debate-how-about-both/

Chapter 5

1   George, Bill (2008). Finding Your True North. Hoboken, NJ: John Wiley & Sons

2   Saltzman, Barry S. (2015, July 13). Why Personal Branding Is Essential To Career Success. Retrieved from https://www.fastcompany.com/3048401/how-to-be-a-success-at-everything/why-personal-branding-is-essential-to-career-success

Chapter 6

1   Lig and Haugen (2000, March) Earnings and Employment Trends in the 1990s. Retrieved from https://www.bls.gov/opub/mlr/2000/03/art2full.pdf

2   Forrester. (2015, April 20). One Million B2B Sales Jobs Eliminated By 2010. (Press Release) Retrieved from https://www.forrester.com/One +Million+B2B+Sales+Jobs+Eliminated+By+2020/-/E-PRE7784

3   Tuli, Aseem (2012, December 19) The B2B Digital Challenge of 2013 (Web log post). Retrieved from https://www.cebglobal.com/blogs/th e-b2b-digital-challenge-of-2013/

4   Taylor, Glenn (2013, December 18) 2013 B2B Buyer Guide Survey: Buyers Happier But Still Waiting To Engage With Sales. Retrieved from http://www.demandgenreport.com/industry-topics/demand-generation-strategies/2456-2013-b2b-buyer-behavior-survey-buyers-happier-bu t-still-waiting-to-engage-with-sales.html

5   LinkedIn (2014) Getting Started With Social Selling On LinkedIn (E-reader Version). Retrieved from https://business.linkedin.com/content/dam/me/business/en-us/sales-solutions/resources/pdfs/linkedIn-getting-started-with-social-selling-ebook.pdf

6   SalesHub (2017) CEO's Guide to The Future of Selling (E-reader Version). Retrieved from https://www.saleshub.ca/the-future-of-selling

7   LinkedIn Sales Solutions (2017). Top Ten Actionable Sales Tips. Retrieved from https://business.linkedin.com/sales-solutions/social-selling/top-10-sales-tips-tricks

8   Henderson, Carl (2016, February 26) 7 Ways to use Twitter for Sales Prospecting (Web log post). Retrieved from https://www.salesforce.com/uk/blog/2016/02/7-ways-to-use-twitter-for-sales-prospecting.html

9.   Brudner, Emma (2015, April 27) Is Social Selling Creepy? Retrieved from https://blog.hubspot.com/sales/is-social-selling-creepy-ne w-survey-report-reveals-what-buyers-consumers-really-think

10 Myerhoff, Alice (2014). Social Media for Sales People (Web log post). Retrieved from https://www.salesforce.com/blog/authors/alice-myerhoff.html

11 LinkedIn (2014) Getting Started With Social Selling On LinkedIn (E-reader Version). Retrieved from https://business.linkedin.com/content/dam/me/business/en-us/sales-solutions/resources/pdfs/linkedIn-getting-started-with-social-selling-ebook.pdf

Chapter 7

1   Foster, Richard (2012) Creative Destruction Whips Through Corporate America. Retrieved from https://www.innosight.com/wp-content/uploads/2016/08/creative-destruction-whips-through-corporate-america_final2015.pdf

2   Dixon and Adamson (2011) The Challenger Sale: Taking Control of the Customer Conversation. New York, NY: Penguin Group.

3   Newman, Daniel (2014, May 7) How Personal Emotions Fuel B2B Purchases. Retrieved from http://www.forbes.com/sites/danielnewman/2014/05/07/how-personal-emotions-fuel-b2b-purchases/#3268972764eb

Printed in the United States
By Bookmasters